WILLIAM
PENN

WILLIAM PENN

Rebecca Stefoff

Introduction by James Scott Brady,
Trustee, the Center to Prevent Handgun Violence
Vice Chairman, the Brain Injury Foundation

Chelsea House Publishers
Philadelphia

Cover: Penn: Archive Photos; Letter: Corbis-Bettman;
  City Hall: © Judy L. Hasday.

Frontis: A bronze sculpture of William Penn watches
  over the city of Philadelphia.

CHELSEA HOUSE PUBLISHERS

EDITORIAL DIRECTOR Stephen Reginald
PRODUCTION MANAGER Pamela Loos
MANAGING EDITOR Jim Gallagher
PICTURE EDITOR Judy Hasday
ART DIRECTOR Sara Davis
SENIOR PRODUCTION EDITOR Lisa Chippendale

Staff for **William Penn**
SENIOR EDITOR Therese De Angelis
ASSOCIATE ART DIRECTOR Takeshi Takahashi
DESIGNER Keith Trego
PICTURE RESEARCHER Patricia Burns
COVER DESIGN Keith Trego

First Printing

1 3 5 7 9 8 6 4 2

Library of Congress Cataloging-in-Publication Data

Stefoff, Rebecca, 1951-
William Penn / Rebecca Stefoff.

112 pp.   cm. — (Overcoming adversity)
Includes bibliographical references and index.
Summary: Focuses on the struggles of the founder of Pennsylvania who promot-
ed the Quaker religion and spent his lifetime preaching the right of each individual to choose his own faith.

ISBN 0-7910-4873-X — ISBN 0-7910-4874-8 (pbk.)
1. Penn, William, 1644-1718—Juvenile literature. 2. Pioneers—Pennsylvania—
Biography—Juvenile literature. 3. Quakers—Pennsylvania—Biography—Juve-
nile literature. 4. Pennsylvania—History—Colonial period, ca. 1600-1775—
Juvenile literature. [1. Penn, William, 1644-1718. 2. Pioneers. 3. Quakers. 4.
Pennsylvania—History—Colonial period, ca. 1600-1775.]
I. Title. II. Series.
F152.2.S85 1997
974.8'02'092—dc21   97-23998
[B]   CIP
                                                             AC

CONTENTS

OVERCOMING ADVERSITY

TIM ALLEN
comedian/performer

JIM CARREY
comedian/performer

BILL CLINTON
U.S. President

JAMES EARL JONES
actor

ABRAHAM AND MARY LINCOLN
political family

WILLIAM PENN
Pennsylvania's founder

ROSEANNE
entertainer

ON FACING ADVERSITY

James Scott Brady

I guess it's a long way from a Centralia, IL, train yard to the George Washington University Hospital Trauma Unit. My dad was a yardmaster for the old Chicago, Burlington & Quincy Railroad. As a child, I used to get to sit in the engineer's lap and imagine what it was like to drive that train. I guess I always have liked being in the "driver's seat."

Years later, however, my interest turned from driving trains to driving campaigns. In 1979, former Texas governor John Connally hired me as a press secretary in his campaign for the American presidency. We lost the Republican primary to a former Hollywood star named Ronald Reagan. But I managed to jump over to the Reagan campaign. When Reagan was elected in 1980, I was "sitting in the catbird seat," as humorist James Thurber would say—poised to be named presidential press secretary. I held that title throughout the eight years of the Reagan administration. But not without one terrible, extended interruption.

It happened barely two months after the Reagan administration took office. I never even heard the shots. On March 30, 1981, my life went blank in an instant. In an attempt to assassinate President Reagan, John Hinckley Jr. armed himself with a "Saturday Night Special"—a low quality, $29 pistol—and shot wildly as our presidential entourage exited a Washington hotel. One of the exploding bullets struck me just above the left eye. It shattered into a couple dozen fragments, some of which penetrated my skull and entered my brain.

The next few months of my life were a nightmare of repeated surgery, broken contact with the outside world, and a variety of medical complications. More than once, I was very close to death.

The next few years were filled with frustrating struggles to function with a paralyzed right side, struggles to speak and communicate.

To people who face and defeat daunting obstacles, "ambition" is not becoming wealthy or famous or winning elections or awards. Words like "ambition" and "achievement" and "success" take on very different meanings. The objective is just to live, to wake up every morning. The goals are not lofty; they are very ordinary.

My own heroes are ordinary folks—but they accomplish extraordinary things because they try. My greatest hero is my wife, Sarah. She's accomplished a lot of things in life, but two stand out. The first has been the way she has cared for me and our son since I was shot. A tremendous tragedy and burden was dropped unexpectedly into her life, totally beyond her control and without justification. She could have given up; instead, she focused her energies on preserving our family and returning our lives to normal as much as possible. Week by week, month by month, year by year, she has not reached for the miraculous, just for the normal. Yet in focusing on the normal, she has helped accomplish the miraculous.

Her other most remarkable accomplishment, to me, has been spearheading the effort to keep guns out of the hands of criminals and children in America. Opponents call her a "gun grabber"; I call her a national hero. And I am not alone.

After a seven-year battle, during which Sarah and I worked tirelessly to educate the public about the need for stronger gun laws, the Brady Bill became law in 1993. It was a victory, achieved in the face of tremendous opposition, that now benefits all Americans. Since the law has been in effect, background checks have stopped 173,000 criminals and other high-risk purchasers from buying handguns, and the law has helped to reduce illegal gun trafficking.

Sarah was not pursuing fame, or even recognition. She simply started at one point—when our son, Scott, found a loaded handgun on the seat of a pickup truck and, thinking it was a toy, pointed it at Sarah.

Fortunately, no one was hurt. But seeing a gun nearly bring a second tragedy upon our family, Sarah became determined to do whatever she could to prevent senseless death and injury from guns.

Some people think of Sarah as a powerful political force. To me, she's the person who so many times fed me and helped me dress during my long years of recovery.

Overcoming obstacles is part of life, not just for people who are challenged by disabilities, illnesses, or tragedies, but for all people. No matter what the obstacle—fear, disability, prejudice, grief, or a difficulty that isn't likely to "just go away"—we can all work to make this world a better place.

In 17th-century England, the Friends—or Quakers—were viewed as a threat to the government and were forced to meet in secret, as this 19th-century photogravure shows. William Penn is portrayed in the center left.

1

A PRISONER
OF CONSCIENCE

ON SEPTEMBER 3, 1667, a group of people converged on a house in the city of Cork on the east coast of Ireland. They gathered quietly and sat on benches and chairs in a large room. Men and women alike were soberly dressed in dark-colored clothing that was simple and plain in style, far removed from the extravagant frills, laces, and ruffles that were the fashion of the time. The men wore hats, which they did not remove when they took their places; the women wore modest head-dresses of white cloth.

Despite their polite manners, these quiet folk were lawbreakers, engaged in a forbidden activity. They were members of a religious group that some people called the Quakers, although they called them-selves the Friends, and they were meeting to worship in their own way: without a priest or a preacher, without a standard service or a ritual, without even a church. Such meetings were illegal; worshiping God was dangerous for the Friends. The British government, which ruled Ireland and England, had outlawed Quaker meetings as a threat to the state. In the eyes of the king and the government, this strange new religion that failed to follow traditional practices was an insult to the established order. In 1660 and 1662 the British legislative assembly, or Parliament, had passed laws that limited the rights of the Quakers and the many other new, nontraditional religious sects that had sprung up in the 17th century. Among other restrictions, these laws made it illegal for more than five Quakers to gather together for what the 1662 act called "pretence of worship." Quakers who defied these laws could be arrested and jailed.

Some communities were more tolerant of the Quakers than others, just as some outsiders respected the Quakers—or at least ignored them—while others mocked and despised them. But although a Quaker meeting was quite likely to be untroubled, the risk of persecution was real. Hundreds of Friends had been arrested, fined, or worse; some had died in prison.

The Friends who gathered in Cork that September day were from many walks of life. Among them were laborers, shopkeepers, and merchants. But one of them came from a different class of society altogether. He was a 22-year-old Englishman named William Penn. His garments were of richer material and were more stylishly cut than those of the other people in the room, and at his hip he wore a sword—something permitted only to the gentlemen of the upper classes.

Young Penn was indeed a gentleman. His father, who owned a large estate near Cork, was an admiral of the British fleet, a war hero, and a friend of King Charles II of England; the young man himself was on friendly terms with the king. William Penn had been brought up by his affectionate but strict father to have a place in court life. He was expected to behave as a traditional English aristocrat should, not to mingle with suspicious religious minorities in outlawed meetings. Yet unknown to Admiral Penn, William had been attending Quaker meetings for half a year. So far he had encountered no trouble, no harassment. But this gathering was different.

The simple, dark-colored clothing and modest headgear of the Friends stood in stark contrast to the frilly, colorful fashions of the 17th century.

A meeting of Friends was unlike the traditional Church of England services that Penn had attended throughout his childhood, the services of other Protestant sects such as Lutherans and Puritans, or the Roman Catholic Mass. The Friends were Christians who believed that God speaks directly to each individual, without need of a special building or a hierarchy of priests and church officials to interpret God's word. All anyone has to do to receive God's message is read the Bible and meditate or pray. Thus

Quaker meetings were sometimes completely silent, as each Friend's thoughts turned inward. Anyone who wished to speak could stand and do so at any time, and speakers often shared their thoughts or experiences, but meetings tended to be tranquil affairs.

The serenity of the September 3 meeting was suddenly broken by clattering footsteps on the stairs. A soldier, loud and ill-mannered and possibly the worse for drink, burst into the room and began bullying the humble Quakers. The soldier felt confident that no Quaker would challenge him, for the Friends honored peace above all things—to be a Friend was to reject all forms of violence, even in self-defense. But William Penn had been brought up with an aristocrat's touchy pride, and he was outraged at such insulting behavior from a common ruffian. He jumped from his seat and advanced on the soldier. One account of the incident says that Penn laid his hand on the hilt of his sword; another version says that Penn grabbed the man by his collar and prepared to kick him downstairs. But before he could act, the horrified Quakers urged him not to commit violence.

Penn now faced his first test as a Quaker. Should he follow the instincts of his upper-class, military background and give the ill-mannered soldier a well-deserved thrashing, or should he follow the Quaker principles that he had recently adopted? After a moment of hesitation, he released his grip on the soldier and let the fellow go. The angry soldier rushed off. In choosing the path of nonviolence, Penn had passed the test of his principles. But another test soon followed.

The soldier returned with a squad of constables and other soldiers. Everyone in the house was arrested and hauled before the mayor of Cork, who was uncomfortably surprised to recognize the son of Sir William Penn in the crowd of prisoners. Hoping to avoid the embarrassment of throwing a lord's son into jail, the mayor announced that Penn had obviously been arrested by mistake, as he

Penn's 1667 letter to the earl of Orrery introduced the concept of separation of church and state. This idea became one of the founding principles of the United States Constitution when the Bill of Rights (shown here)—the first ten amendments to the Constitution—was adopted in 1791.

could not possibly be a Quaker. He added that Penn was free to go.

This was Penn's second test, and he passed it without hesitation. Stepping from the prisoner's dock to the mayor's bench, he said loudly and clearly that there had been no mistake. He was a Quaker.

Penn then insisted upon being charged with the same crimes as the other Quakers. He said that because he had studied law, he would defend himself and his fellow Quakers against the charges. And by the way, he asked the flustered mayor, just what were those charges?

The mayor responded that the Quakers were charged with rioting and holding an unlawful assembly under the 1660 law. Penn argued that the true purpose of that law had been to protect the state not against Quakers but against another new sect called the Fifth Monarchists, whose religious beliefs were linked to plans to overthrow the English government. The Quakers posed no such danger, he explained, and therefore should be exempt from the law.

Such subtle reasoning was beyond the mayor. He ordered all the Quakers, including Penn, thrown into jail. Legend says that Penn paused at the door of the jail, unbuckled his jeweled sword, and handed it to a puzzled but grateful bystander, announcing that he had given up fighting forever. No evidence supports this persistent story, but perhaps it is true; other events in Penn's life suggest that he was capable of grand, impulsive gestures.

Once he and his fellow Friends were in jail, Penn's first action was to send for pen, ink, and paper. He wrote a letter to the earl of Orrery, who was the president of Munster, the part of Ireland where Cork is located. The earl could overrule the mayor's decision to jail the Quakers—and he also happened to be a friend of Penn's father.

This letter was the first of many documents that Penn was to write about an issue that became the central focus of his life: freedom of religion. Instead of simply pleading for justice for himself and his friends, he called for tolerance toward all religions. He declared that a person's relationship with God should be regulated not by kings or mayors but by the individual's own conscience, and he wrote defiantly, "Religion, which is at once my crime and my innocence, makes me a prisoner to the Mayor's malice, but mine own free man." Penn reminded Orrery that the Quakers were nonviolent and posed no political threat. Then he went a step further, suggesting that the state had no right to favor one religious sect over another. This idea—that church and state should be separate—was considered extremely unsound and dangerous in 1667. Later it was to become one of the founding principles of the United States Constitution.

Whether or not Orrery was impressed with Penn's plea for liberty and toleration is unknown. Perhaps he simply wanted to get his friend's son out of prison. Whatever the reason, however, he ordered that Penn and the other 18 Quaker prisoners be set free. William Penn's experience in Cork was the first time that he was jailed for his beliefs, but it would not be the last. Only a few years later he would be considered a dangerous political prisoner and thrown into solitary confinement in the notorious Tower of London.

Penn would suffer other hardships as well, including money problems, betrayals by friends, and stormy relationships with his father and with his own sons. Yet he would also experience great successes: triumphs of the spirit, if not always worldly glories. He would win respect for his courage as a spokesperson for the Quakers. He would become the owner of the largest private property ever possessed by anyone not of royal blood. And he would have the rare privilege of turning his dreams into reality by founding the colony of Pennsylvania.

But while Penn is often remembered simply as the founder of Pennsylvania, he was much more than that. He was one of the first thinkers to ponder deeply the question of individual rights and to speak and write on behalf of those rights. In Britain and throughout Europe, he fought against injustice and prejudice. His long crusade for religious toleration helped change the laws of Britain, bringing greater liberty of conscience to all. Long after his death, his beliefs and practices helped shape the new nation of which Pennsylvania became a part.

The Penn family crest, with the motto "Dum Clavum Teneam"("As long as I hold the helm"), a fitting phrase for a family of sea merchants.

2

BORN INTO TROUBLED TIMES

THROUGHOUT HIS LIFE, the founder of Pennsylvania was proud of his ancestry. The Penn family name was an old and honorable one in England. Although William Penn claimed to be related to a family named Penn in the county of Buckinghamshire that could trace its ancestry to a Norman knight of the 11th century, genealogists—historians who specialize in the study of family trees—have not been able to prove a connection between the Buckinghamshire Penns and the founder's own family.

The Quaker William Penn's family can, however, be traced several generations back to a prosperous farmer, also named William Penn, who owned a large estate in Gloucestershire, a county in central England. This ancestral Penn died in 1591. His son, another William, was a law clerk. Among the law clerk's six children was a son named Giles, who became a merchant sea captain. Sailing out of Bristol, a trade port on England's southwest coast, Giles Penn made himself into an important personage. He traded with the Spanish, Moroccan, and Algerian merchants and pirates who controlled the western part of the Mediterranean Sea, and because he learned Arabic and made friends among the Moors and Algerians, he was able to obtain Arabian horses and hunting falcons, which were highly prized throughout Europe. By making gifts of these horses and falcons to members of the English aristocracy, Giles Penn gained influence at court. He was appointed to the post of English consul, or diplomatic representative, in the Moroccan city of Salé. One of his principal duties was ransoming English captives who had fallen into the hands of Arab pirates.

Giles Penn planned a lucrative career in commerce for his sons, George and William. But George, who had married a Spanish woman, fell afoul of the Spanish authorities for unknown reasons and was thrown into prison in Seville. He was eventually released, but he was ordered never to return to Spain; this ruined Giles Penn's hopes of a family trading company with branches in Spain and England. Giles's other son, William, was the father of William Penn the Quaker. Giles Penn had meant for this son, who at an early age was an experienced seaman, to captain the merchant vessel that was to make the family's fortune. William Penn's career took a different direction, however. He chose a military rather than a mercantile career.

The mid-17th century was a time of great turmoil in England. Certain factions of the public grew increasingly dissatisfied with the rule of King Charles I, who had ascended the throne in 1625. Many people, particularly the officers and soldiers of the country's army, were beginning to feel that the king had too much power and that England's Parliament should have a greater say in running the country. A rift developed between the monarchists, or Royalists—who supported the absolute rights of the monarch—and the antimonarchists, or Parliamentarians—who favored reducing the king's powers and strengthening those of Parliament.

Religion and politics were closely intertwined in the 17th century, and religious differences played a great part in the upheavals of English government and society that occurred in the middle of the century. The Church of England (also called the Anglican Church) had been the country's official religion since the early 16th century. There were some Roman Catholics in England, but they were regarded with distrust and were often persecuted, as were Presbyterians. Also persecuted were the members of new Protestant sects outside the Anglican Church: these individuals were labeled Separatists, Nonconformists, or Dissenters because they declared their faiths to be separate from the officially recognized church, because they failed to conform to Anglican practices, or because they dissented from—that is, disagreed with—Anglican doctrine.

Even within the Church of England, however, there were factions. One group of Anglicans, called the Puritans, wanted to change, or purify, the church from within. The Puritans called for an end to practices that resembled those of Roman Catholics—for example, they felt that the system of bishops and archbishops should be abolished. They felt that the church, like society in general, had become preoccupied with showy, superficial effects and had lost sight of simple godliness. Eventually some Puritans, unable to come to agreement with the mainstream of the Anglican Church, fled the country; among these were the first settlers of the Massachusetts colony in North America. Other Puritans eventually left the ranks of the Anglicans and joined the Nonconformists. But the Puritan movement within the Church of England remained strong, and over time the Puritan and Parliamentarian causes became linked, largely because the king and the aristocracy were vigorously opposed to the idea of Puritan reforms. Most Puritans were Parliamentarians, and many Parliamentarians were Puritans. Thus the war between the Royalists and the Parliamentarians was partly a religious controversy.

War in England was preceded by strife in Scotland and Ireland, both of which had come under English rule. Pres-

Penn's father, Admiral Sir William Penn. Like that of his son, Sir William's loyalty to the British government was questioned on several occasions, and he was jailed under suspicion of plotting against those in power.

byterianism had been the religion of Scotland for two centuries, yet Charles I tried to force the Scots to adopt Church of England practices. At the same time, unrest broke out in Ireland, where Roman Catholicism was the dominant religion. The Irish resented the land-grabbing dominance of the English. When in 1642 a clash between King Charles and Parliament broke out into open civil war, the Irish sided with the king and the Scots sided with Parliament. The parliamentary soldiers, most of whom were Puritans, were nicknamed Roundheads because they wore their hair cropped short. Royalist forces continued to favor the long, curled hair and wigs that had been fashionable under King Charles; they were called Cavaliers. Led by a Puritan general named Oliver Cromwell, the Roundheads quickly took control of London. Before long, they had the Cavaliers on the run.

Around this time, Giles Penn's son William joined the navy. Various accounts exist about how his naval career began. Some say he joined the Royal Navy in 1641, while the king was still in power, hoping for advancement because his father stood high in the court's favor. Others say he joined in 1642, after the king had lost control of London and the navy to Parliament. In any case, William Penn's private sympathies were with the Royalists, and historians have debated his motives for serving the Parliamentarians. One possibility is that he felt a duty to remain in the navy so that he could serve his country regardless of who ruled it. Another, less idealistic, explanation is that he saw how quickly the Parliamentarians won the upper hand and decided it would be wise to stay on good terms with the party in power. At any rate, William Penn was 22 years old when the English Civil War broke out. The Parliamentarians seemed to have had no doubts about his loyalty: almost at once he was given command of a ship in the parliamentary navy. His vessel, the *Fellowship*, was part of a squadron sent to patrol the waters off Ireland to keep the rebellious Irish Catholics from sending aid to the Royalists.

Captain Penn returned to London whenever he had shore leave, and there, in 1643, he met a young widow named Margaret Jasper Vanderschuren, whose background remains something of a mystery. She came from a Protestant family of English, Irish, or Dutch origin, and she had been brought up in Rotterdam in the Netherlands. While still a teenager, she had married a Dutch merchant named Nicasius Vanderschuren, who took her to live in Ireland. It is unknown whether they had children, although it is unlikely; there is no mention in the Penn family records of any children by Margaret's first husband. Nor is it known when or how Margaret's first husband died. We

The 19th-century French artist Paul Delaroche created this dramatic and fictional scene of Oliver Cromwell surveying the body of Charles I. The execution of Charles I sent most Royalists into exile, where they plotted to defeat Cromwell.

After Margaret Penn, William's mother, lost her family's Irish property to the Royalists during the 1641 rebellion, Admiral Penn was granted this property in County Cork, Ireland, as compensation. The Penns moved to Macroom Castle, shown here, in 1657.

do know that by late 1641, when the Catholic uprising broke out in Ireland, Margaret was a widow. She fled to London with her parents to escape the turmoil in Ireland. Still quite young and by all accounts a lively, merry, good-natured woman, she soon caught the eye of Captain Penn. They were married in June 1643.

The Penns rented lodgings on Tower Hill, a fashionable neighborhood almost in the shadow of the state prison called the Tower of London. On October 14, 1644, their first child was born. They named the boy William. Although Captain Penn's ship was already on its way to Ireland, the captain himself had remained behind to be present at the child's birth. As soon as the boy was baptized—at a small, medieval church called All Hallows Barking on Tower Hill—Captain Penn took to his horse and galloped off to rejoin his ship, which had stopped along the coast. He would not return home for more than a year.

Throughout young William's childhood, in fact, his father was away at sea, except for brief visits home. The elder Penn rose to the rank of admiral, but he was plagued by troubles. While on duty in Ireland, he became friendly with an aristocrat named Lord Broghill, who was known to sympathize with the Royalists. This friendship made Cromwell and the Puritans start to question Penn's loyalty to the parliamentary government. In 1648 Penn was thrown into jail under suspicion of being a Royalist plotter. Nothing was proved against him, however, and Cromwell, who knew that the navy could not afford to lose one of its best commanders, ordered him released within a month. But rumors about Admiral Penn persisted. Some of his enemies whispered that he had Royalist leanings; others claimed that he lacked courage, drank too much, or diverted into his own pocket some of the money he was given to buy food and other supplies for the men in his command. Admiral Penn later became a war hero, but these rumors haunted him throughout his naval career.

The admiral's fortunes rose steadily for a few years, during which England continued to be shaken by momentous events. The most dramatic of these events occurred in January 1649, when Charles I, who had been captured by the Puritan forces sometime earlier, was beheaded by order of Parliament. At a time when monarchs were thought to be almost godlike and many people still believed that the touch of a royal hand could cure illness, Charles's execution was an earthshaking deed. It outraged the Royalists, of course, but even some people who had supported the Parliamentarians began to feel that the zealous Puritans had gone too far. Many Royalists, including most of the surviving Cavaliers, fled England for the Netherlands. While in exile there, they set up a court with Charles II, son of the murdered king, as its head, and they began brewing plots to defeat Cromwell.

For the time being, though, the Puritans were firmly in power in England and Cromwell was in charge. After the king was beheaded, England was declared to be a new nation, the Commonwealth, with Cromwell as its leader. A few years later Cromwell took the title Lord Protector of the Commonwealth. One of his main goals was to strengthen England against its enemies abroad—both foreign forces and exiled Royalists. Admiral Penn proved useful in this task. He scourged the Irish coast, pursued fleeing Royalist vessels into the Mediterranean, and went to battle at sea against the Dutch fleet when war broke out between England and the Netherlands in 1653. The commander of the Dutch fleet, Admiral van Tromp, fastened a broom to the highest mast of his flagship, vowing to "sweep the English from the sea." But it was the Dutch who were mopped up, and much of the credit went to Penn, whose men grappled van Tromp's own ship and tore the hated broom from the mast. Penn was rewarded with a gold chain from the lord protector.

Finding himself high in Cromwell's favor, Penn asked for a grant of land to make up for the loss of his wife's Irish property, which had been seized by the Royalists. The Puritans in turn had confiscated some Royalist lands in Ireland, and Cromwell gave Penn a parcel of it—an estate called Macroom, located near Cork. Cromwell also appointed Penn to command a fleet that was being sent to capture the Spanish colony of Hispaniola in the Caribbean Sea (the island that today is divided between the nations of Haiti and the Dominican Republic).

While Admiral Penn was making a name for himself on the high seas, his son, William, lived a quiet life at home. The Penns no longer lived in crowded, dirty London. Admiral Penn thought London was too unhealthful for his family, especially after young William suffered an attack of smallpox that caused all his hair to fall out. So the admiral had moved his wife and son and their servants to a residence near the village of Wanstead, 11 miles from London. The Wanstead home was really a farm, large enough to produce its own supply of vegetables, dairy goods, and

livestock; these were valuable considerations because the war had disrupted farming throughout the land and provisions were in short supply in London and elsewhere. The move from the city to the green, open country of Wanstead made a powerful and favorable impression on young William, who became a passionate gardener in later life and always maintained that country life was far superior to city life. "The Country is both the Philosopher's garden and his Library, in which he Reads and Contemplates the Power, Wisdom, and Goodness of God," William would write in 1693.

William later claimed that he had never wasted time in playing, and indeed it seems as though his childhood was rather earnest. Popular activities such as sports, plays,

The Chigwell Free Grammar School in Chigwell, County Essex, where young William studied until the family's move to Macroom Castle in Ireland.

fairs, and circuses had been outlawed by the Puritans, who viewed them as worldly frivolities. Rowdy games and pastimes were frowned upon. Children were expected to be serious little people and to spend all their time studying, working, or praying. And although Margaret Penn was a fun-loving woman who was far from strict, William seems to have been a naturally quiet and studious child. His only known recreation was running footraces. He greatly enjoyed his father's visits home on leave; other visitors included his grandfather Jasper and his uncle George, who told hair-raising tales of his imprisonment in a Spanish dungeon. For the most part, however, the household consisted only of William and his mother until 1652, when William's sister Margaret (called Pegg) was born. Four years later the Penns had a third child, a boy they named Richard, or Dickie.

If William had friends or playmates among the Wanstead boys, they have been forgotten. But one childhood acquaintance was destined to play a significant part in William's life: a girl named Gulielma Springett, or Guli. A few months older than William, Guli lived in Wanstead with her mother and stepfather. Admiral Penn and his family knew Guli's family, including her stepbrother, Isaac Penington, who was a Quaker—probably the first that William Penn met.

Little is known about William's early education. As a youngster on Tower Hill he may have been tutored at home or in a small private academy; no record of such teaching remains. But somehow he learned to read. By the time he was 11 years old he could read and write English and Latin; he also knew a little French and Greek. William loved reading and appears to have read widely, even as a child, but historians do not believe that Admiral Penn's household contained much of a library. Perhaps William borrowed books from tutors or family friends.

William's first known formal education began when he was enrolled in the Chigwell Free Grammar School at age

11. The school was located in the village of Chigwell, about four miles from the Penns' home, and William ran back and forth between home and school six days a week. Mondays through Saturdays, classes began at six in the morning and lasted for 10 hours in summer and 8 in winter, with an hour off on Thursdays and Saturdays to play. Chigwell was a private academy—there were no public schools in England. Only boys whose parents could afford to pay for tuition were able to attend. And like nearly all schools of the time, Chigwell was closely connected with the Church of England; in fact, it had been founded by an archbishop. William's school days thus included plenty of prayers and psalms along with lessons in grammar and history.

The Chigwell boys studied the writings of ancient Greeks and Romans whose works were considered sober and virtuous. Modern English writers—including the playwright William Shakespeare—were banned as vulgar and bawdy. All lessons were taught in Latin, and the pupils were supposed to answer questions and give recitations in Latin as well. Any boy who slipped up and spoke English in class was whipped by the schoolmaster. This rigorous program appealed to young William—or at least he said years later that it had. He described himself as being "of a retired temper" and claimed that he "could never join" in his classmates' games and pranks. His closest friend at Chigwell was the Latin teacher. At this time, William was also becoming interested in religion. He spent many hours alone reading his Bible, and he also read books and pamphlets by churchmen. He even came across some of the works of John Saltmarsh, a religious mystic who had once lived in Wanstead. Saltmarsh had written several booklets calling for religious liberty. In letters written a few years later, between 1668 and 1674, William said that in 1656 or 1657, while reading his Bible and Saltmarsh's essays, he was sometimes filled with a great sense of peace and holiness: "The Lord appeared to me," he explained. He entered

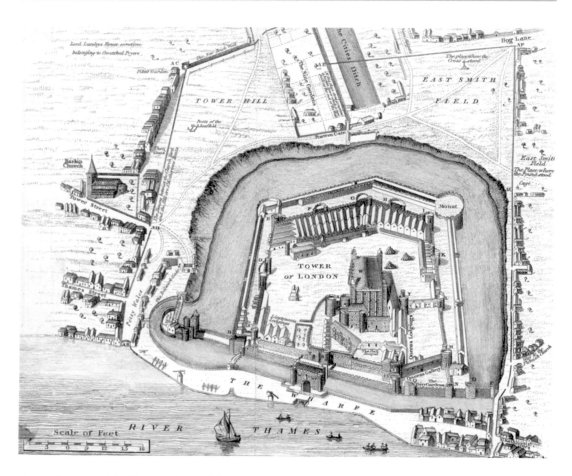

An early map of the Tower of London, where both Admiral Penn and his son William were imprisoned for various offenses against the government. Tower Hill, where William Penn's parents first lived after their marriage, is shown here in the upper left.

his teens with strong religious feelings.

William's life was abruptly shaken out of its familiar course when a crisis occurred in Admiral Penn's career. The expedition that Cromwell had sent to the Caribbean failed to capture Hispaniola. The failure was not the fault of Admiral Penn, who commanded the ships and sailors; the expedition's soldiers, commanded by General Robert Venables, had been beaten back by heat, hunger, and disease as much as by the Spanish garrison. Unwilling to return to England empty-handed, Admiral Penn took the fleet to Jamaica, another Spanish-occupied island in the Caribbean, and captured it. Cromwell was furious. The lord protector was a tyrant who expected his orders to be followed to the letter, and even though Jamaica was a richer prize than Hispaniola, he complained that the expedition's leaders had not done what he had told them to do. Upon their return to London, Venables and Penn were thrown into the Tower of London. The official reason for their imprisonment was that they had come home without orders to do so, but there were rumors that Penn had secretly offered to turn the whole fleet over to Charles II.

Once again, nothing could be proved against Admiral Penn, and he was released from the Tower after only five weeks. But he was now tainted by the suspicion of Royalist sympathies. The navy stripped him of his command and forced him to retire. Penn's downfall was both humiliating and terrifying for young William, who took great pride in his father's rank and heroism. It was an early lesson in the fickleness of fame and fortune—a lesson that William was to learn again, when he, too, was unjustly imprisoned.

After his release from the Tower, William's father decided to move his family to his Irish estate, hoping that he could support the household on the rents paid by his tenant farmers. In 1656 William was taken out of school, and the Penns crossed the Irish Sea to settle at Macroom.

Macroom Castle was a large, square, three-storied tower of gray stone; outside the castle walls was a village where the tenant farmers lived. William's family spent four years at Macroom. The house was usually full of friends and family members, including William's cousin, Uncle George's son, who was also named William. The admiral was both angry and melancholy about his fall from grace, and to cheer himself up he surrounded himself with relatives and seafaring cronies. Sadly, he also began drinking heavily. His son, meanwhile, pursued his studies at home, perhaps with the help of a tutor, and for recreation he and his cousin rambled through the nearby moors and fields.

Young William may have met some Quakers during this

time, either at Macroom or in the city of Cork, 26 miles away, where a small meeting, or congregation, of Friends had been established. Nearly 40 years later, Penn told a story about the visit of a well-known Quaker to Macroom Castle. He said that his father had heard of a man named Thomas Loe who had converted many people in Cork to Quakerism. The admiral broadmindedly invited Loe to visit Macroom, where Loe delivered a speech on the Inner Light—the Quaker belief that God resides in every man's and woman's soul and that every person can commune directly with God. This moving speech brought tears to the eyes of all listeners, from the crusty admiral to Anthony, the family's black slave.

Some scholars have suggested that perhaps Loe never really visited Macroom. They point out that throughout his life, Admiral Penn gave no evidence of being interested in religion, nor of being tolerant of Nonconformist sects. And no record exists of the visit except in William Penn's much later reference, written at a time when he may have been confused about the past. If the visit did occur, Loe's speech may have laid the groundwork for William's own conversion to Quakerism some years later.

After the Penns had been at Macroom for four years, events in the Commonwealth took a new direction. Oliver Cromwell died in 1658. His son, Richard, who succeeded him as lord protector, proved so weak and ineffective that he was nicknamed "Tumbledown Dick." Soon the country was in chaos. Cromwell's iron dictatorship had turned many against the Puritans, and now people across the country were beginning to call for the end of the Commonwealth and a return to the monarchy. Scores of plots arose to restore Charles II to the English throne. No one knows for certain what part, if any, Admiral Penn played in these conspiracies, but he is known to have been in contact with Royalist supporters. Early in 1660 he moved back to London. When a new parliament was formed, Admiral Penn was elected to it, along with many other

Royalists. In April the new parliament voted to invite Charles II to return, and Admiral Penn—once more in the thick of public affairs after four years of bitter isolation in Ireland—was a member of the delegation that was sent to the Netherlands to bring back the king.

The Protestant seminary at Saumur, France, where William Penn studied under Moïse Amyraut from 1662 to 1664. Amyraut's views on the importance of individual conscience in discerning divine truth greatly influenced Penn's own religious beliefs.

3

THE
YOUNG SEEKER

KING CHARLES II returned to England in grand style. The ship that carried him, christened the *Naseby* after a battle that Cromwell had won, was immediately rechristened the *Royal Charles* as the king stepped aboard. Once on the ship, Charles summoned Admiral Penn and dubbed him Sir William Penn, knight of the realm. Most historians believe that Penn must have given substantial aid to the Royalist cause to be rewarded in this way.

The monarch's triumphant return marked an upswing in the fortunes of the Penns. The Royalist who had owned Macroom before the Penns received it demanded its return from the king. In exchange, Charles gave Sir William an even larger Irish estate called Shanagarry, also near Cork. Furthermore, Sir William was appointed to a high-paying job as commissioner of the Royal Navy. He settled his family in a large new house in a section of Tower Hill where many naval officers and administrators lived. The Penns' neighbor was Samuel Pepys (pronounced "Peeps"), secretary of the navy's supply department, who kept a long and detailed diary describing the people and events of his time. Pepys's

Much of what we know about the young William Penn and his parents appears in the diary of the English politician Samuel Pepys. Although never intended for the public eye, Pepys's diary has become a classic in English literature.

diary, one of the most colorful sources of information about 17th-century London, contains many references to the Penn family. Pepys disliked all the Penns. He claimed that Margaret Penn was fat and dowdy and that her cooking "stank like the Devil." He thought young William was a conceited little prig. And he once wrote of Sir William, "I hate him with all my heart." Yet, like many bureaucrats, Pepys was skilled at hiding his true feelings and making himself agreeable to those in power. "Out of great and necessary discretion," as he described it, he passed himself off for years as a friend of the Penns.

Sir William and Lady Margaret embarked on a period of high living, with frequent riotous parties at which everyone drank heartily and engaged in crude practical jokes. Young William held himself aloof from these festivities, preferring to read in his attic bedroom. In the fall of 1660 he set off for Oxford, a university town north of London, for the next stage in his education. He was 16 years old, and his father had decided that he needed to acquire some polish and make friends among the well-born, newly restored Royalists.

Sir William enrolled his son in Christ Church, one of the most aristocratic colleges in Oxford. Penn was not an ordinary student. He held the rank of gentleman scholar, which meant that he was not really expected to work hard or to take his education seriously; he was one of 20 young men from noble or influential families who had special privileges and were thought to add prestige to the college. But William Penn was quite unlike the other gentlemen scholars of his time. His earnestness and his failure to do what was expected of him would enrage Sir William—and not for the last time. Penn's stay at Oxford marked the beginning of a long period of friction between the serious, idealistic young Penn and his conventional, ambitious, fierce-tempered father. In his own quiet way, William Penn was becoming a rebel.

Penn arrived at Oxford just as England was entering a period known as the Restoration because the Stuart dynasty, the royal family to which Charles I and Charles II belonged, had been restored to the throne. The Restoration was a free-spirited, pleasure-loving time, during which people reacted with glee to the lifting of Puritan restrictions. Theaters opened, and playwrights such as William Congreve produced witty comedies about romance and seduction. Poetry, music, and dancing, which had been outlawed by the dour Puritans, flourished during the Restoration. The Puritans had dressed in drab clothing, but during the 1660s, men and women alike wore fur capes, silk stockings, and clothing of bright blue and green satins and velvets decorated with ruffles, ribbons, and bows. The new freedom of the Restoration caused some people to go a bit wild; many wealthy young men thought of little but drinking, chasing women, brawling, and fighting duels. The king himself set a notorious example with many scandalous love affairs.

Penn did not really have the Restoration spirit. He had friends among his highborn, frivolous fellow students, but he was not satisfied by their pastimes. As a lonely, studious child reading his Bible, he had developed a deep spirituality that remained with him and grew even stronger once he entered the busy, worldly life of the university. Penn was searching for a sense of purpose or significance in his life, for enlightenment, and he privately felt that Oxford was "a signal place for idleness, loose living, profaneness, prodigality, and gross ignorance," filled with "hellish darkness and debauchery."

Penn had hoped that college would bring him into contact with other minds like his own—minds that had been formed by wide reading and that were eager to study and debate weighty questions of religion, philosophy, and politics. Although he did not find such intellectual companions among the jolly Cavaliers, he did meet a few kindred spirits at Oxford. The foremost of these was Dr. John Owen, a Puritan religious scholar who had been vice-chancellor of the university. When the Stuarts were restored, the Puritans fell into disfavor and the more traditional element within the Anglican Church returned to power. Owen was dismissed from his university post, but he continued to live just outside of Oxford, and he welcomed visits from students who wanted to discuss religion in an atmosphere of open-minded tolerance.

Owen encouraged his young followers to question the authority of the established church. An unusually free-thinking man for his time, he felt that the university should be a place for fair and unprejudiced debate, where students could examine new ideas—including the ideas of the Quakers and other Nonconformist religious groups who were generally scorned by both mainstream Anglicans and strict Puritans. William Penn became acquainted with Owen and began visiting his house on Sundays with a few like-minded young men. Owen greatly influenced Penn. Through his friendship with the older man, Penn learned to organize his thoughts and express his opinions—and also to respect free inquiry. John Owen did more than anyone else to help shape William Penn the writer and crusader for liberty.

In April 1661 Penn made his first visit home to London, covering 57 miles by stagecoach in one and a half days. A grand public celebration was planned to celebrate the coronation of Charles II, and Sir William wanted his son by his side. The Penns and the Pepyses went together to a rented room overlooking the route that the king and his procession would follow. The pageant was lavish. "So glorious was the show with gold and silver," wrote Pepys,

Christ Church in Oxford, England, where William Penn attended college as a "gentleman scholar." Here Penn met Dr. John Owen, perhaps the most important figure in his intellectual life.

"that we were not able to look at it, our eyes being so much overcome." Sir William swelled with pride when both King Charles and his brother, James, the duke of York, waved to him in greeting.

Penn started his second year at Oxford in the fall of 1662, and soon afterward Sir William began to worry about his son. He learned from the college authorities that William, along with several other young men, had stopped attending the chapel services that all students were required to attend. Instead, Penn and his friends were holding their own services at Dr. Owen's home. The authorities had warned the boys to stop visiting Owen, who was con-

Although Admiral Penn was not openly a Royalist, his fortunes improved when Charles II, shown here in a 17th-century engraving, was restored to the British throne. The Penns were granted an Irish estate called Shanagarry and Sir William received a prestigious and lucrative commission in the Royal Navy.

sidered a bad influence on their discipline and values, but the boys continued to call on their mentor. This defiant behavior puzzled and angered Sir William. He had intended for Penn to have all the social advantages of a fashionable education, and now the boy was demonstrating contempt for the way things were done. In January 1662 Sir William called Penn to London for a confrontation.

The meeting between father and son was awkward. Sir William was a domineering man of definite opinions, not likely to show much patience for anyone who disagreed with or defied him. And although most young people at times simmer with rebellion against their parents, Penn was becoming something more than an ordinary rebellious teenager. He was turning into a young man of independent mind who insisted on thinking for himself. Sir William thought this was a dangerous trend and gruffly ordered his son not to do anything that would make him stand out from the crowd. The admiral also began to think about transferring Penn from Oxford to Cambridge, another university, where the boy would be out of Owen's circle.

Before he returned to Oxford, Penn spent an afternoon alone roaming through London. At the docks he saw a ship being loaded for its voyage to the American colony, and he had what he later described as an "opening of joy," a moment of religious insight when he realized that in the New World across the ocean, people could live and think in new and freer ways. Years later, he would test this idea by founding Pennsylvania.

Penn went back to Oxford, but he did not stay long. He was appalled by the false religion of many of the teachers and students, who piously attended chapel every day and then went home to commit as many sins as they could. He felt that it was hypocritical to profess to be a Christian but not live like one. So he continued to follow his conscience, ignoring the university chapel services and meeting with Dr. Owen to pray and discuss religion. Then, in March, he went home to London and announced that he had been expelled from Oxford.

Historians are puzzled by Penn's description of his expulsion. The records of Christ Church list every one of the students expelled over the generations, but Penn's name is not among them. Penn later said that he had been "banished" from Oxford for writing a book that criticized the established church. No such book or record of its existence has ever been found. Today, most scholars agree that when Penn described his departure from Oxford—years after it happened—he had either knowingly exaggerated or had made a mistake. More likely, Penn probably just withdrew from the college in disgust and frustration.

It must have been difficult for Penn to tell his father that he was not going back to school. Sir William did not receive the news gracefully. According to Penn's own account, Sir William beat him and turned him out of the house. Penn was able to come home a few hours later, but the gossipy Pepys noted in his diary that the boy looked quite unwell and that father and son appeared to be on bad terms with one another.

Hoping that a change of scene would snap the boy out of his odd religious mood, Sir William sent Penn to France. In July 1662, traveling with the earl of Crawford and several other young noblemen, Penn crossed the English Channel and made his way to Paris.

The admiral's plan almost worked. Europe was exciting, and Penn was caught up in the sights and sounds of a new environment. For a few months he lived the typical life of a wealthy Englishman in Paris: having stylish new clothes made by the best tailors, seeing sights such as the cathedral of Notre Dame, and copying the elaborate manners of the members of the French court. Among other things, he learned about a new fad in France: the napkin. (One brand-new etiquette manual said that every gentleman should know 27 ways to fold a napkin.) Once he had mastered court etiquette, Penn was presented to King Louis XIV—a sign of tremendous social success. Soon, however, a shocking incident changed the course of his life and drove him back to the spiritual quest he had begun at Oxford.

Late one night, as Penn was returning through the dark Paris streets to his lodgings, a harsh voice rang out. A man suddenly ordered Penn to defend himself. The belligerent stranger said that he had just walked past and had taken off his hat to Penn. By the rules of etiquette Penn should have taken off his own hat in return. This custom, called "hat honor," was a courtesy practiced among gentlemen, and the stranger was insulted that Penn had not observed it. He challenged Penn to a sword fight. In vain, Penn explained that in the shadowy street he had not even seen the man pass and that he meant no discourtesy. The man drew his sword. There was a brief clash of arms and Penn, through luck or skill, disarmed his opponent. Now the advantage lay with Penn. He had been challenged, and he had won. He would be within his rights, as they were understood by gentlemen of the time, if he ran his opponent through the heart. Instead, Penn picked up the man's fallen sword, handed it to him with a bow, and walked on.

The encounter lasted only a few minutes, yet it lingered in Penn's thoughts for a long time, troubling him. What kind of "honor" caused men to fight to the death over the raising of a hat? "I ask any man of understanding or conscience if the whole round of ceremony was worth the life of a man," Penn wrote. He was perplexed and full of questions, and he decided to leave Paris and look for the answers. His search took him to Saumur, a small Protestant seminary, or religious college, on the Loire River in central France. One of the leading professors at Saumur was Moïse Amyraut, a lawyer turned teacher, who claimed that any man or woman could understand God's laws by studying his or her own heart. Amyraut's beliefs, in fact, were close to those of the Friends. It is not known how Penn happened to come to Saumur; perhaps his friend John Owen had advised him to study with Amyraut.

In any event, Penn spent a year or more at Saumur. Although he was not formally enrolled in the seminary, he lived in Amyraut's house and followed a course of reading laid out for him by the liberal professor. In long discussions about the Bible, historical events, and current political affairs, Penn sharpened his insights and his debating skills. He also devoted considerable time to prayer and quiet meditation. He felt himself moving further and further away from the conventional doctrines of the Church of England, but he did not yet identify with any other faith. He knew only that he was searching for a form of worship that placed more value on individual conscience than on priestly hierarchy.

Amyraut died in 1664, and Penn left Saumur. Back in

The Parliamentarian Algernon Sidney remained exiled from England from 1659 until long after Charles II was restored to the throne. A fierce advocate of nonconformists, Sidney's views on government by the people intrigued the young Penn.

Paris he met a former Oxford classmate, Robert Spencer, the future earl of Sunderland. Spencer proposed that they travel together to Italy, and Penn eagerly agreed. He had a wonderful time on the trip, delighting in the mild, almost tropical warmth of southern France and the grandeur of the Alps. But when the two men reached the city of Turin in northern Italy, Penn found a message from Sir William. England and the Netherlands were about to go to war, said Sir William, and Penn was to come home at once while he could still do so.

On his way home, Penn met Algernon Sidney, an Englishman living in exile in Europe. Sidney believed that England should be a republic and that ordinary people should choose their leaders. Such republicanism was dangerously radical at the time, and Charles II would not allow Sidney to spread his ideas in England. But Penn was stimulated by his conversations with the political theorist. Along with his meditations on religion and conscience, Penn now began to consider whether government ought to be by the free consent of the governed, rather than by force or tradition.

In August 1664 Penn arrived in London after an absence of two years. Sir William and Lady Margaret were pleased to see their son clad in bright, fashionable clothes, using graceful French manners, and speaking knowledgeably of King Louis and other European notables. But Samuel Pepys confided sourly in his diary that Penn had "a great deale, if not too much, of the vanity of the French." He added, "I fear all profit he has made in his travels will signify little."

By now Penn was nearly 20 years old. We do not know for certain what he looked like. None of the few portraits that exist was painted from life; they are all copies of originals that are now lost. But from various descriptions, we do know that Penn was considered tall and that he became stout as he grew older. His hair was probably light brown and his eyes were large and dark. He wore his hair in long locks, but it was thin, possibly as a result of his childhood bout with smallpox. On the whole, he was a presentable young man, and Sir William hoped that he would reach great heights at court. The admiral decided that the next step in Penn's education should be the study of law. He did not really expect his son to become a lawyer, but the London law colleges, called the Inns of Court, were like Oxford—a place for a young man to rub elbows with other sons of the rich and powerful. In February 1665, therefore, Penn was enrolled in Lincoln's Inn, an ancient and prestigious law school.

But Penn's time at Lincoln's Inn was short. Before the end of his first semester, he was called away by his father. England and the Netherlands were once again at war, and Admiral Penn was going to sail against the Dutch fleet as he had done in the heroic days of 1653. This time, however, William was no longer a small boy waiting anxiously at home to hear the outcome of the battle. This time, William Penn was going to battle too.

Within the image: ÆTIS. 22. 1666. OCTOBER.14   PAX QVÆRITVR ~BELLO~

This image of a youthful William Penn clad in armor is one of many copies of an original painting commissioned by Penn himself. Penn had decided to become a soldier shortly before he attended his first Quaker meeting.

4

IRELAND AND
THE QUAKERS

IRONICALLY, THE MAN who later became a pacifist enjoyed his first experience of war. Penn was neither a soldier nor a sailor, and he was not an officer; he was a volunteer aide to his father. In those days, many young gentlemen went to battle in this informal way in order to acquire martial glory. Sir William, who dreamed of a high-level court appointment for his son, wanted Penn to accompany him so that the young man could meet and make a good impression on James, the duke of York, who was lord high admiral of the English fleet. As the great captain commander, Sir William officially took orders from the duke, but in reality he commanded the fleet himself, for James lacked the experience to do so. Penn was part of Sir William's staff on the flagship *Royal Charles*, where he met James, the king's brother. The two remained on good terms for many years.

Penn liked life aboard ship and even showed signs of interest in a naval career. But he did not remain on the *Royal Charles* for long. After only a month or so, Sir William sent his son back to London to carry secret dispatches, or papers, to the king. Charles II received the

Penn met the Duke of York, who would later assume the crown as James II, while serving under his father in the Royal Navy. After James's conversion to Catholicism sometime between 1668 and 1671, Catholics and other nonconformists enjoyed unprecedented religious liberties.

dispatches in person and held a short conversation with Penn, during which he praised Sir William and asked about his welfare. This episode seems to have impressed Penn mightily. He felt a new admiration and affection for his father after seeing him in command of a fleet and respected by royalty.

But Penn did not return to the *Royal Charles*. Sir William had acccomplished his mission—introducing his son to the king and the duke of York—so he directed Penn to return to Lincoln's Inn and resume his studies. Penn dutifully wrote to Sir William: "As I never knew what a father was until I had wisdom to praise him, so can I safely say that now, of all times, your concerns are most dear to me. 'Tis hard meanwhile to lose both a father and a friend." The relationship between father and son, so often turbulent, had become closer and warmer.

As it happened, Penn was back at Lincoln's Inn for just a few weeks before a dire emergency closed the law school. London was in the grip of bubonic plague, a virulent epidemic of a disease that was also called the Black Death. The plague, transmitted by fleas that were carried from city to city by rats, had ravaged Europe several times in the past. In the 14th century it killed a quarter of the population of the continent, and in 1625 another outbreak claimed the lives of 40,000 Londoners. In 1665, just as the Dutch and English fleets were maneuvering for battle, the Black Death struck again. The Great Plague of London killed more than 100,000 people between the spring of 1665 and December of that year. At the height of the plague, 7,000 died weekly, and corpse-haulers trundled carts through the city, mournfully chanting, "Bring out your dead." Those who could do so fled the pestilent city for the countryside. London became a ghost town, occupied only by the poor, the dying, and the criminals who preyed upon them. The city would suffer a second devastating blow in September 1666, when it was swept by the Great Fire, the worst conflagration in London's history.

The fire destroyed four-fifths of the city.

One result of the plague and the fire was an increase in the activity of Nonconformist religious groups, many of whom preached that God was punishing the city for its sins. The Quakers did not promote this blood-and-thunder belief, but they were much in evidence during the disasters, for many of them remained in the city to nurse the sick and help the homeless. The plague also stirred Penn's thoughts about the impermanence of human life. He later wrote, "In the time of the Great Plague of London, the Lord gave me a deep sense of the Vanity of this World, of the Irreligiousness of the Religions in it."

Although the Penn family survived the plague, they faced other problems. The English fleet had defeated the Dutch in battle on June 3, but the English had unaccountably failed to follow up this victory by pursuing the fleeing Dutch vessels and wiping out the whole enemy fleet. The duke of York, who had not ordered pursuit, was officially to blame for this failure, but Sir William Penn stepped forward to take the blame, allowing people to think that he had advised the duke against pursuit. In this way, the king's brother was spared harsh criticism.

Sir William, however, received plenty of criticism. Old accusations of cowardice and drunkenness were revived, and once again Sir William's enemies whispered that he had pocketed money that should have been spent on supplies for his men. The Stuarts were privately grateful that Sir William had saved the duke from embarrassment, but they thought Sir William should withdraw from the public eye for a time. So the hot-tempered sea captain, who had begun to suffer from the painful disease of gout, returned home to London. The plans he had made to request an appointment to the navy staff for his son were postponed. Instead, he sent Penn to Ireland on business related to the Shanagarry estate.

Penn arrived in Ireland in January 1666. After finishing his duties at Shanagarry, he went to Dublin and fell in with a lively set of sophisticated young men who spent their time discussing art, flirting with the local belles, and gossiping about their acquaintances among the nobility. Recalling this period, Penn later admitted, "The glory of the world was with me, and I was ever ready to give myself to it." Penn not only experimented with novel social distractions, but also sought a second taste of military adventure.

When mutiny broke out among some English soldiers stationed in Ireland, Penn was among a number of gallant gentlemen who voluntarily joined forces to quell the revolt. The mutineers were quickly overcome, and Penn, excited by the victory, decided to become a soldier. Around this time he had a portrait of himself painted, in which he appears as a young, wavy-haired man with a gentle but somber expression, clad in dark armor. The original portrait has been lost, but three copies of it, made in the 18th century, survive. They are thought to be the closest we have to an accurate image of Penn.

Penn was offered the captaincy of a garrison in Ireland, but Sir William ordered him not to accept it. The admiral may have been pleased that his son was showing an interest in the manly art of soldiering, but he did not want Penn to be buried in an insignificant Irish command. "He shall dig potatoes first," the indignant Sir William declared. He thought a captaincy was not good enough for his son, for whom he envisioned a glorious career at court. The relationship between father and son again grew strained, with Penn chafing against his father's strict control. Before long, however, events turned Penn away both from the army and the court.

He was in Cork one day when he happened to chat with a shopkeeper there—some accounts say that he recognized her from his time at Macroom years before. She was a Quaker, many of whom made their livings as owners of shops and small businesses. Customers liked dealing with them because, unlike most merchants, the Quakers did not haggle or bargain over prices. Instead, they set a fixed price for their goods and charged everyone the same amount, because they believed it was important to practice fairness and equality in everyday matters.

According to Penn's account of this encounter, he mentioned that he had once heard a Quaker named Thomas Loe speak, and he added that he would gladly travel a hundred miles to hear him again. No need to go so far, the woman replied. Loe was in Cork to attend a Quaker meeting. Penn was welcome to come and hear him there, if he wished. Penn promised he would do so.

Whether or not he had really heard Loe at Macroom, Penn was apparently curious about the Quakers. He kept his promise and attended the meeting, where Loe spoke eloquently on the idea that "there is a faith which overcomes the world and a faith which is overcome by the world." Penn was deeply impressed by a faith that remained true to its inner convictions, regardless of the rules and limitations placed upon it by bishops and kings. He later said of his experience, "the Lord visited me with a certain sound and testimony of his Eternal word." The Friends used the word "convincement" to describe Penn's experience: the moment when someone is suddenly filled with a profound inner certainty of God's presence. In Quaker terms, Penn was convinced that day in Cork. At last he had found what he had been searching for ever since his childhood, when he pored over his Bible and tried to understand God's will. He declared that he intended to join the Friends.

This was a momentous decision, even a dangerous one. The Friends were subject to much persecution, and by associating with them Penn risked similar treatment. As he spent more time with his new Quaker friends, Penn learned that they had had trouble with government authorities from the start.

Quakerism was an outgrowth of a mass religious movement of the 17th century during which people

The only known likeness of George Fox, the founder of the sect originally known as "Children of Light." Today, members of the Religious Society of Friends are commonly called Quakers.

throughout Europe pulled away from their established churches. In England, Puritanism gained strength and scores of entirely new sects sprang up. Among these were the Ranters, the Diggers, the Levelers, the Baptists, the Seekers, the Muggletonians, the Fifth Monarchists, and many more. Most of these Nonconformist or Dissenting groups preached a simplified form of Protestantism, stripped of tradition and priestly show. They emphasized the individual and the importance of seeking truth through one's own conscience. Some of these sects vanished almost as suddenly as they had appeared; others established their places in history.

One of those caught up in this religious ferment in 1643, a year before Penn was born, was a young man named George Fox. Dismayed by people who attended church regularly but still lived sinful, greedy lives, Fox wandered from sect to sect in search of a faith that would unite the spiritual and the worldly. Gradually, he began speaking about his own beliefs and won followers. By 1652 his followers, who called themselves the Children of Light or the Friends of Truth, had become a significant sect. Their chief principles were that God speaks directly to any heart that opens itself to hear (this was called the doctrine of the Inner Light), that formal churches and preachers are unnecessary, and that people should live as Jesus Christ did, reflecting in every action their inmost beliefs. The Friends stressed simplicity, fairness, and equality. Because they believed that no person is inherently better than any other, they refused to perform the customary hat honor and they also used the terms "thee" and "thou" instead of "you" when speaking to others (at that time "thee" and "thou" were used only to address servants, children, and social inferiors, while people of superior standing were addressed as "you"). These egalitarian practices irked many wellborn people, and the Friends' rejection of the established religion was a thorn in the side of both the state and the church. The Quakers often got into

trouble because they refused to pay tithes, or church taxes, to the Anglican Church and also because they refused to take oaths—that is, to swear to something on God's name.

The term "Quaker" came into use early in the movement. Some people said that the Friends were called Quakers because they trembled, or quaked, with intense feeling during their meetings. Fox himself said that the name was coined in 1650 by a justice of the peace when Fox warned the official to "tremble at the Word of the Lord." Whatever its origin, the name was soon adopted, and before long it was no longer considered an insult; many Quakers, including William Penn, used it to refer to themselves. But they continued to call themselves Friends, and they addressed one another as "Friend Fox," "Friend Penn," and so on. Today the worldwide community of Quakers is

The Friends met with persecution not only from the Church of England, but also in New England by the Puritans, as shown in this engraving. Ironically, the Puritans themselves traveled across the sea to North America in search of religious freedom.

A follower of George Fox is publicly flogged in the streets of England.

called the Society of Friends, a name that came into use in the late 18th century.

The Quakers were misunderstood, feared, and hated by many people. Some people disliked the Quakers simply because they were different—they dressed plainly, spoke modestly, and seemed to live outside of conventional society. Although their beliefs were somewhat similar to those of the Puritans, the Quakers were persecuted as viciously by intolerant Puritans as they were by traditional Anglicans. Indeed, four Quakers were hanged in Boston by the Puritans—who had themselves fled to Massachusetts to find religious freedom. Both the Commonwealth and the Restoration periods were difficult for the Quakers as well as for other Nonconformists. Laws were passed forbidding free speech and assemblies for such groups. One prominent Quaker, James Naylor, was convicted of blasphemy in 1656 for preaching his religious views; his punishment was to have a hole burned through his tongue with a red-hot poker. Between 1650 and 1689, thousands of Quakers were thrown into prison and as many as 450 of them died there. Following one's conscience against the rest of the world is always difficult, but in the 17th century it was heroic.

Penn's enthusiasm was unquenched by the fear of persecution. He was young and vigorous, ready—and even eager—to overcome obstacles for his newfound faith. The teachings of John Owen and Moïse Amyraut had led him to believe that everyone should be free to think, pray, and worship in his or her own way.

Penn began attending Quaker meetings in Cork and other communities in eastern Ireland. The meetings were held in secret to avoid harassment or arrest. But these precautions failed on September 3, 1667, when the rowdy soldier interrupted the Friends meeting in Cork, leading to Penn's arrest—and to his declaration that he was a Quaker. Penn's letter to the powerful earl of Orrery brought the release of all the Quakers from the Cork jail, but another hurdle lay ahead: Penn had to face his father.

Orrery wrote to Sir William, telling him what his son had been up to in Ireland. The admiral was furious that Penn had gone so far as to identify himself with an outlaw sect. He wrote the following letter from the Navy Office on October 12, 1667. "Son William," it began,

I have writ several letters to you since I received any from you. By this I charge you strictly and command that you come to me with all possible speed. In expectation of your compliance, I remain, Your affectionate father, W. Penn.

Penn did not respond at once, claiming that he still had business to attend to at Shanagarry. On October 22 the impatient admiral wrote again:

I hope this will find you in health. The cause of this writing is to charge you to repair to me with all possible speed, presently after your receipt of it, and not make any stay there, or any other place on the road, until it pleases God you see me (unless for necessary rest and refreshment). Your affectionate father, W. Penn.

In other words, Penn was to drop everything and come home at once, pausing only to sleep and eat. But Penn did not depart for London until December, and then he did not go alone. One of his new acquaintances, a Quaker named Josiah Coale, came with him—a circumstance that was not likely to delight Sir William.

Indeed, the gout-ridden admiral, already facing a formal impeachment on charges of embezzling naval funds, was in no mood to humor his son's religious fancies. One dramatic version of their meeting says that Penn threatened to throw himself out of a window rather than renounce his Quakerism, but this colorful tale is based only on legends and there is no reliable account of it. What is known, however, is that Sir William ordered Penn to give up his Quaker nonsense, that Penn refused, and that the admiral reacted with anger and deep disappointment. He must have felt that the boy was deliberately throwing away the fine future for which the admiral had worked so hard to prepare him. But to Penn, the matter was one of conscience and integrity. Having found his faith, he would not be shaken.

Not only did Penn continue to call himself a Quaker,

but he also attended meetings of Friends in and around London. Already he was defining a role for himself among the Friends. Better educated—and certainly better connected—than most of them, he would become their foremost spokesperson. George Fox, Thomas Loe, and others were brilliant speakers, but the movement lacked a writer who could explain and defend Quakerism and record its history and development for future members. Penn filled that role. And with his contacts in high places and his smattering of legal knowledge, he would leap to the defense of Quakers who were arrested or persecuted.

During the first few months of 1668, relations between Penn and his father were strained almost to the breaking point. Penn was frequently away from home on Quaker business. The charges against the admiral were dropped and he returned to work at the Navy Office. But he was unable to celebrate; he was worried about his son. Then, Penn was arrested again. This time the magistrate refused to imprison him, but he told Sir William to give his son a warning. Enraged at this public humiliation, Sir William ordered Penn to move out of the house, declaring that he would leave his estate "to them that pleased him better." It seemed that the rift between these two stubborn souls had finally widened beyond all hope of mending.

Imprisoned several times for his religious and political beliefs, Penn used the time to write a number of important treatises on individual freedom, including his explication of Sandy Foundations Shaken, *which he titled* Innocency with Her Open Face *(1669), and* The Great Case of Liberty of Conscience *(1671), a defense of toleration.*

5

TRIALS

PENN THREW HIMSELF into his new life as a Quaker. Although he remained in touch with his family, he now traveled and lived with other Quakers. In July 1668 he toured the country with Coale and Loe, urging others to join the Quakers. Penn's strength was in attacking vanity and the false pleasures of worldly goods. Even though he still wore better clothes than his fellow Quakers and had not removed the fancy plume from his hat, he was now considerably more drab in appearance than most gentlemen of the period. In his talks, he tore into those who prided themselves on their lavish dress, saying, "How many pieces of ribbon, feathers, lace bands and the like had Adam and Eve in Paradise or out of it?" He demanded to know whether the Virgin Mary had used face powder or worn "false locks of strange colours." On this tour he also met George Fox, with whom he would later become friends. Much of what we know about Fox's character and actions comes from Penn's writings.

The tour led the traveling Quakers though Buckinghamshire, where they called on Penn's childhood acquaintance, Gulielma Springett.

Penn wrote the most important of his works, No Cross, No Crown, *while imprisoned in the Tower of London. The treatise defends Quaker doctrines and practices, and criticizes the un-Christian behavior of England's clergy.*

135

N O
Crofs, no Crovvn :
Or feveral Sober
R E A S O N S
Againft
Hat-Honour, *Titular-Refpeas*, *You* to a
fingle Perfon, with the *Apparel* and
Recreations of the Times :

Being inconfiftant with Scripture, Reafon, and the
Praaice, as well of the beft Heathens, as the holy Men
and Women of all Generations ; and confequently
fantaftick, impertinent and finfull.

With Sixty Eight Teftimonies of the moft famous Perfons,
of both former and latter Ages for further confirmation.

In Defence of the poor defpifed *Quakers*, againft
the Praaice and Objeaions of their Adverfaries.

By W. Penn *j.*
An humble Difciple, and patient Bearer of the
Crofs of Jefus.

But Mordecai *bowed not*, Efth. 3. 2.   Adam *where art thou !* Gen. 3. 9.
In like manner the women adorn themfelves in modeft Apparal, not
with brodered hair, &c. 1 Tim. 2. 9. *Thy Law is my Meditation all*
the day, Pfal. 119. 97.

Printed in the Year, 1669.

Like her stepbrother, Isaac Penington, she had become a Quaker. After this visit, Penn and Gulielma began corresponding. Penn addressed her as Guli and also signed his letters Guli, a shortened form of Gulielmus, which is Latin for William.

Penn's role as a spokesman for the Friends resulted in his imprisonment in the Tower of London in late 1668. A Presbyterian minister named Thomas Vincent had been attacking the Quakers in violently offensive speeches, and Penn—who had matured as a debater under the tutelage of

Owen and Amyraut—challenged Vincent to a public debate at which both sides could present their arguments. Vincent agreed, but he insisted that the debate be held in his own chapel. When Penn and his fellow Quakers arrived, they found the building filled with Vincent's noisy supporters. Vincent spoke first, and he spoke for hours— one source says he prayed aloud until after midnight. As soon as he finished, he and his followers trooped out, leaving Penn no chance to respond.

Vincent then published a pamphlet called *The Foundations of God Standeth*, in which he continued his attack on the Friends. Stung to anger, Penn wrote a reply called *Sandy Foundations Shaken*. Unfortunately, it was hastily written and included some language that was interpreted as an attack on the established church and the state, although such things were far from Penn's intention. Some highly placed persons in the Church of England declared that *Sandy Foundations Shaken* was blasphemous—that is, that it undermined official church doctrine. Because the king of England was also the formal head of the Church of England, an attack on the Church was also considered an attack on the state, and blasphemy could also be interpreted as treason. Penn was thrown into the Tower under suspicion of both.

At first he was held in solitary confinement in a cold, dismal cell. After a week or so, he received a message from the archbishop of London stating that unless he admitted to blasphemy and apologized for it, he would remain in prison until he died. Penn replied that he had committed neither blasphemy nor treason and would not apologize, for he had done nothing wrong. "My prison shall be my grave before I will budge a jot, for I owe my conscience to no mortal man," he is said to have responded.

A week or so later, Penn was moved to better quarters and his servant, Francis Cooke, was permitted to bring him fresh clothing. The archbishop then sent Edward Stillingfleet, the bishop of London, to reason with Penn.

But the plan backfired when Penn and Stillingfleet became friends. Although neither could fully accept the other's views, they liked and respected one another, and their debates were probably the most pleasant feature of Penn's jail term.

Penn was also able to write letters to Guli and other friends and to work on more religious pamphlets. The most important of these was a treatise called *No Cross, No Crown*, in which Penn called for a return to the simplicity and purity of early Christianity, before faith became cluttered up with ritual and pomp. Over the years, Penn revised and expanded *No Cross, No Crown* several times, and it became one of his most influential and enduring works.

Meanwhile, efforts were under way to release Penn from prison. Sir William wrote to the king's council pleading for his son's release and lamenting that Penn's Quakerism had been "a great affliction." (Unknown to Penn, Sir William had softened somewhat toward his wayward son and had drawn up a new will that left him the bulk of the Penn estate.) At the same time, Penn himself moved on two fronts. First, he petitioned the king for release, saying that he had been imprisoned without a fair trial, which was every Englishman's right. Second, with Stillingfleet's help, he wrote a pamphlet called *Innocency with Its Open Face*, in which he explained that *Sandy Foundations Shaken* had been aimed not at the Church of England but only at Vincent—a Dissenter who was highly critical of the established church.

Penn's release on July 28, 1669, was probably the result of all these factors. He was set free after seven and one-half months in the Tower. In the eyes of the Quakers, he was now a hero and martyr who had proved his commitment to their cause. But to many outside the Quaker movement, controversy and imprisonment had tainted Penn. There were even rumors that he was a Catholic spy—a serious accusation at a time when Protestant England was rabidly hostile toward Catholic nations such as France and

Spain and many Englishmen feared Catholic plots to take over their country.

Although the Stuarts had Catholic sympathies (the duke of York was a practicing Catholic), they wanted to allay the fears of the Protestant Parliament, so they enacted strict anti-Catholic laws and allowed Catholics to be cruelly persecuted. Somehow the notion entered the public mind that Penn might be mixed up with the Catholics. People hinted that he refused to raise his hat because he had the shaven head of a Catholic priest. Or perhaps the "Saumur" where he claimed to have studied was really St. Omer, a well-known Catholic seminary. These rumors were utterly false and ridiculous, but Sir William nevertheless thought it best to keep Penn out of the mainstream of London society for a time, so he sent Penn back to Shanagarry. Intending to devote all his time to writing and missionary work, Penn hired a Quaker colleague named Philip Ford to serve as the steward, or manager, of the estate. He would regret this decision years later.

On their way to Ireland, Penn and Ford stopped to visit Guli Springett; some accounts say that Penn and Guli became engaged during this visit. Then the two men crossed the Irish Sea, reaching Cork in October 1669. Penn found that many Quakers had been imprisoned in Ireland, and through persistent visits to high-ranking authorities—who could not turn him away for fear of offending Sir William—Penn was able to get them released. He returned to England in June 1670, leaving Ford in charge at Shanagarry.

Later that summer Penn and other Quaker leaders decided on a bold plan to prove that Quaker meetings were not political conspiracies and should be legalized. Penn announced that he and William Mead, another prominent Quaker, would hold a public religious meeting, in violation of strict new laws. When police constables barred the doors of the meetinghouse, Penn and Mead convened their meeting in the street. The constables began to arrest them

Gulielma Springett married her childhood friend William Penn in 1672. The Penns had six children, including sons Springett and William and daughter Letitia as well as three others who died in infancy. Guli Penn died in 1694.

on charges of preaching in a public thoroughfare. A scuffle broke out in the crowd, and the charge was changed to the much more serious one of inciting a riot. Penn and Mead were brought to trial before Sir Samuel Starling, the lord mayor of London, on September 3, 1670.

Starling was not an impartial justice. He ordered the court bailiffs to snatch Penn's and Mead's hats, then fined the two men for failing to remove their headgear in court. He made disparaging remarks about Penn's father, calling him "Sir William who starved the sailors." He would not let Penn, who was acting as lawyer for Mead and himself, cross-examine any of the witnesses. But Starling's hostility toward the two Quakers backfired. Such obvious and heavy-handed malice offended the jury and tilted the jurors in favor of the defendants. When the verdict was delivered, Mead was found innocent, and Penn was found guilty only of preaching in the street.

The verdict provoked an uproar. Sir Samuel angrily ordered the jurors to reconsider. They did so, but delivered the same verdict. Then Sir Samuel declared that he would hold them without food and drink until they found both defendants guilty of inciting a riot.

Penn's trial was already important to his fellow Quakers. Now it took on a grave importance for all the people of England. The very heart of England's judicial system was the concept of trial by jury, and suddenly the freedom of jurors to deliver a verdict without bullying or fear of reprisals was threatened. The jury's foreman, Edward Bushell, clearly saw the significance of the occasion. He fortified the resolve of the other jurors, and although the lord mayor held them prisoner for two days without food or access to toilets, they did not waver. Instead, when Sir Samuel called them back into court, expecting an obedient verdict of "guilty on all counts," the jurors announced that they now found *both* defendants innocent on all counts. The vindictive mayor fined each juror for contempt of court. They all refused to pay. So Sir Samuel ordered them

all to Newgate Prison—the dirty, crowded, disease-infested prison of debtors and common criminals—and sent Penn and Mead to Newgate along with them.

Sir William was distressed to see his son in jail again, this time in a filthy commoners' prison. For a change, he agreed with Penn's principles, but he urged his son to pay his fines and get out of jail. The admiral was gravely ill and was afraid he would die without seeing his son again. Penn said that he could not give in and pay, so the admiral secretly paid for both Penn and Mead, and the two Quakers were released. Eight jurors also paid their fines, but Bushell and three others staunchly refused. They were released on bail two months later, and when they came to trial for contempt, the lord chief justice of England upheld their case. In effect, the outcome of the trial was a confir-

A typical Quaker meeting at Jordan Meeting House, near Chalfont St. Giles in Buckinghamshire, England, where Guli Springett and William Penn worshiped. Serene gatherings such as this were viewed as treasonous by the British government until James II assumed the throne.

mation of the jury's right to make an independent decision. Scholars of the law hail this case as a landmark in judicial history, and the real credit goes not to Penn or Mead but to Edward Bushell, the jury foreman, who would not save himself by letting the judge bend the law.

Penn left Newgate just in time for a final meeting with his father. The admiral still did not approve of the course Penn had chosen, but he loved his son and hoped to part from him on good terms. He died a week after Penn was released from prison. After his father's funeral, Penn wrote a pamphlet called *Truth Rescued from Impostors* defending Sir William against the rumors and suspicions that had haunted the elder man's career.

His long struggle with his father was over, and Penn had inherited a great deal of money. He was readier than ever to devote himself to full-time Quaker activity. His polished speeches and writings attracted many converts to the Friends. Among them were rich or highborn men and women who were willing to listen to Penn but who would have disregarded Fox or Loe, who were self-educated commoners. Before long, though, Penn was arrested again, and he was sentenced to six months in Newgate for refusing to swear an oath.

As before, Penn used the time in jail to write, producing an important work called *The Great Case of Liberty of Conscience*, which calls for both religious toleration and political rights. Its underlying principle is that people are basically reasonable beings who will naturally make the right decisions about worship and government; therefore they should be left free to worship as they please, and they should have a greater voice in the government.

Upon his release from Newgate in August 1671, Penn made a second trip to Europe. This time he headed not for the glittering festivities of Paris but to the Netherlands and Germany, where he met with members of other Noncon-formist groups and tried to make converts for the Friends. (Fox and a few others had just sailed across the Atlantic to

America on a similar mission.) But Penn's trip was unsuccessful and he wanted to see Guli, so he returned to England in October. There he was asked to take on many of Fox's responsibilities for organizing the Friends and maintaining communication among meetings in different parts of the country.

Fox returned from America in 1673, but after a few months he was arrested and imprisoned under the provisions of a law called the Test Act, which required people to swear allegiance to the king. Constables and magistrates had taken to arresting Quakers on trivial charges and then, before dismissing them from court, asking them to swear the oath of loyalty. When they refused to use God's name to swear an oath, the Quakers were imprisoned for violating the Test Act. Fox remained in jail until 1675. During

Worminghurst Place in County Sussex, England. The Penns moved to this estate, which Guli inherited from the Springett family, in 1676.

Fox's imprisonment, Penn once again took on many of the tasks of Quaker leadership.

Penn also assumed more personal responsibilities. He married Guli Springett on April 4, 1672, and the couple settled in a town called Rickmansworth in southeast England and started a family. It was not uncommon in the 17th century for children to die in infancy; sadly, Penn's first three children met this fate. Penn's brother, Richard, also died around this time while visiting Penn. Fearing that Rickmansworth was unhealthful, Penn moved his family to an estate called Worminghurst in the open countryside of southern England just after his fourth child, a son named Springett, was born. This child survived the perils of infancy.

In 1677 Penn went back to Europe, this time accompanied by George Fox and other Friends. Traveling through the Netherlands, Belgium, and Germany, they met with religious leaders and made further missionary efforts to attract converts. Although few of those with whom they spoke actually joined, the Friends found that most people listened courteously and with interest—which must have been heartening, given the hostility the Friends often met at home.

Penn's family continued to grow in the following years. His daughter, Letitia, was born in 1678, and a son, William Jr., was born in the spring of 1680. By this time, Penn had become involved with an American venture. In 1674 he was asked to settle an argument between two English Quakers, John Fenwick and Edward Billinge, over the ownership of the southern part of the New Jersey colony, which they had bought from Lord Berkeley, the colony's proprietor (a proprietor held rights to a colony as a grant from the Crown). After reviewing the case, Penn decided that the property in question belonged to Billinge, who was deeply in debt. To raise money toward his debts, Billinge offered tracts of land to colonists willing to settle in the New World. Penn was one of the administrators of this colony. He and Billinge hoped to build a Quaker settlement there, and in 1677 they launched the settlement with 230 colonists. Penn also advised Billinge to draw up a charter of rights and freedoms for the colonists. Among other rights, this charter guaranteed freedom of religion and government by the people—foreshadowing some of the most important provisions of the United States Constitution.

Penn's involvement with the Billinge colony turned his thoughts toward America. He remembered the "opening of joy" he had felt years earlier when he watched a ship set sail for the New World. Although Quakers had been present in the American colonies almost since the beginning of their movement, they had encountered little toleration there. Now Penn began to think about starting an entirely new colony as a Quaker sanctuary. This was the genesis of Pennsylvania.

William Penn (right) receiving the Charter of Pennsylvania from Charles II in 1681.

6

THE HOLY EXPERIMENT

PENN'S MUSINGS ABOUT a new colony in America took a great leap forward in 1679. Until that year, Penn had optimistically believed that reform was possible in England and that, given the chance, people would create a more progressive, liberal government that allowed liberty of conscience and protected individual rights. When the political philosopher Algernon Sidney came out of exile in 1679 to run for Parliament, Penn was overjoyed. He had admired Sidney since meeting the older man in Europe years before. Sidney stood for everything Penn hoped to see in a public figure.

But Sidney was soundly defeated, and Penn himself was forcibly thrown out of the local polling place. He began to fear that parliamentary reform was impossible. Dejected, he concluded that all around him immorality was flourishing while virtue was being persecuted. From this time on, he believed that the New World offered the best chance for reform.

With money at his command, a social status that gave him access to most important people in the country, and a persuasive tongue and pen,

William Penn set out to win a grant of land from King Charles. He knew that Charles had owed a substantial sum of money to Sir William Penn and that the debt had not been repaid. Penn decided to approach the king by suggesting that a land grant would cancel the old debt to his father. Furthermore, he would point out that if a large number of Quakers settled in America, as Penn hoped they would, the Quakers would no longer be troublesome in England—for which the king should be grateful. Penn presented these arguments to carefully chosen allies in the royal court, and he accompanied them with discreet bribes—for he was not above using underhanded means to achieve such an important goal. One of his allies was the duke of York, who had always liked Penn. Another was Robert Spencer, the earl of Sunderland, with whom Penn had once toured France and Italy; Sunderland was now the king's secretary of state. He notified Penn when the king was in a favorable mood, and on June 1, 1680, Penn formally petitioned Charles for the large tract of land west of New Jersey, sandwiched between New York and Maryland. A richly wooded, fertile region, the land was cut by numerous rivers, with rolling hills in the east and rugged mountains in the north and west. Both Coale and Fox had seen the territory and had spoken of its beauties.

Years often passed before such petitions were granted or rejected, but in Penn's case the decision was made quickly, probably because Penn had generously bribed the right people. When it came to naming the new colony, however, disagreements arose. King Charles wanted to name it Pennsylvania, or "Penn's Woods," not after Penn himself but after his father the admiral, who had been instrumental in Charles's return to the throne. Penn did not like this idea. He was sure that his critics would think he had named the colony after himself and would accuse him of vanity. He asked Sir Leoline Jenkins, one of the king's counselors, to dissaude Charles from adopting this name. Unfortunately, Penn's suggestion, New Wales, named after

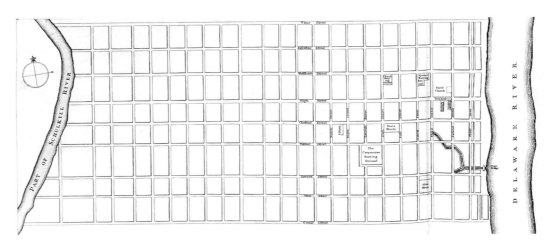

a hilly and wooded region in western England, offended Sir Leoline, who happened to be from Wales and was affronted at the comparison with a barbaric land inhabited by savages (the conventional English upper-class view of America and Native Americans). Leoline refused to raise the matter with the king, and the name Pennsylvania stood.

On March 14, 1681, King Charles II signed a document called the Charter of Pennsylvania. In return for a token annual rent—two beaver skins and one-fifth of any gold or silver that might be discovered on the land—Penn became the sole proprietor of the largest territory ever owned by a private British citizen. Only one individually owned colony in all of recorded history has ever been larger, and that was the Belgian Congo, which was the personal property of King Leopold II of Belgium during the late 19th century.

As proprietor, Penn's powers were sweeping. He could appoint officials and make laws. (Although in theory those laws had to be approved by officials in London, in practice the proprietors were rarely questioned.) He was required to allow a Church of England clergyman to establish a church in Pennsylvania if 20 or more colonists requested it, but this provision did not bother Penn, since he planned to offer complete religious freedom to all. In fact, he called

An engraving (c. 1752) of the gridlike street plan devised for the city of Philadelphia by William Penn and his surveyor general, Thomas Holme. Such advance planning was unique for its day; the pattern was copied by many towns and cities as America expanded westward.

the establishment of Pennsylvania a "Holy Experiment" in which he would attempt to embody God's will in an earthly place. Believing that God intended all men to live together in harmony and mutual toleration, Penn hoped to achieve these conditions in Pennsylvania. The colony was to be a sort of utopia, a Greek word meaning "no place" coined by Sir Thomas More in his 1516 book about an ideal and imaginary world. Penn intended—with God's help—to turn his version of utopia into reality.

One of Penn's first acts was to appoint his cousin William Markham as deputy governor. Markham sailed for Pennsylvania to begin building relationships with the Native American peoples who lived there and also with the thousand or so Europeans who had already settled in Pennsylvania. Most of these settlers were Dutch and Swedish, the remaining settlers from earlier colonizing ventures. Penn invited them to stay, and many of them did. These earlier settlers were the first of what would be the large and long-standing Dutch and Swedish communities of eastern Pennsylvania.

Penn also tried to attract settlers from Europe, chiefly from France, Germany, and the Netherlands. A number of Germans from a region called the Palatinate eventually did answer his call; most had met Penn or had heard him speak during his missionary tours. They formed the nucleus of a thriving German community in Pennsylvania. The community that is now called "Pennsylvania Dutch" was actually German in origin—the English colonists mistakenly called the Palatinate Germans "Dutch," and the name was handed down.

Penn was less successful in attracting colonists from France. He had hoped that French settlers would bring their silk-making and wine-making skills to Pennsylvania and establish industries there, but few French families came. He was pleased, nonetheless, that at least some colonists came from the European continent to join the Welsh, English, Scottish, and Irish settlers in the colony.

"THY GOD BRINGETH THEE INTO A GOOD LAND OF FOUNTAINS AND DEPTHS THAT SPRING OUT OF VALLEYS AND HILLS A LAND WHOSE STONES ARE IRON AND OUT OF WHOSE HILLS THOU MAYEST DIG BRASS"

st's view of Penn the Welcome. *Penn companions did not England for America eptember 1, 1682, more year after Penn was d the land.*

He wanted people fr
amicably as part of
slow at first, but th
until by 1683 or 1
bringing more mem

To Penn's deligh
craftspeople and co
been afraid that th
who would settle o
ized that farming w
in Pennsylvania, h
that was partly u

Penn drew up The Frame of the Government *for Pennsylvania to insure that he and his successors would have "no power of doing mischief, so that the will of one man may not hinder the good of a whole country." A new frame of government, the* Charter of Privileges, *superseded it in 1701.*

Penn was a pioneering city planner who had spent a great deal of time visualizing his ideal city.

Painfully familiar with London and other European capitals where plague spread quickly through crowded slums and fires sometimes ravaged whole districts in a matter of hours, Penn wanted his capital to bring the healthfulness of country life into the city—an entirely new blend of both ways of life that he described as "a greene countrie towne, which will never be burned, and always be wholesome." Instead of narrow, twisting alleyways, he planned broad, tree-lined avenues running in a grid pattern along straight lines from north to south and from east to west. He included many parks, marketplaces, and squares, and each building would stand in the center of a lot containing a garden or orchard. Penn's capital, which he named Philadelphia (meaning "the city of brotherly love"), was the first American city to be laid out in advance, and its unique design was later emulated by many towns and cities as America's frontier moved westward.

In addition to city planning, Penn also engaged in social planning. He had many ideas that he wanted to put into practice in Pennsylvania. For one thing, he determined, all children from age 12 would be taught useful trades or skills. He also guaranteed the right of juries to return verdicts without fear of harassment—a lesson he had learned from his own trial with William Mead. Penn's own experiences also influenced his rules for imprisonment: all prisoners were to be treated well and provided with food and heat. And certain behaviors and activities, such as drunkenness, cursing, gambling, stage performances, lying, and gossiping were prohibited throughout the colony.

From these restrictions, we can see that Penn's idealistic belief in individual freedom sometimes came into conflict with his equally strong conviction that he knew the right way for others to live. He was so certain that his own ideas were best that he could not always resist the temptation to impose them upon others. This quality was evident in the constitution, which outlined how the colony would be governed. Three offical bodies were established in Pennsylvania: the governor (Penn), the Council, and the much larger General Assembly. Members of both the Council and the General Assembly would be elected by the vote of all adult male residents (women were not permitted to vote). Penn drew criticism from other liberal thinkers, such as Algernon Sidney, who asserted that Penn's arrangement, in which the Assembly could approve or reject laws proposed by the Council but could neither debate those proposals nor propose laws on its own, would weaken the Assembly, the larger and therefore more representative house of the legislature. And some Quakers pointed out that, as governor, Penn had reserved three votes for himself, while everyone else was permitted only one vote each; this scarcely meshed with the notion of universal equality. Others were disappointed that Penn had not outlawed slavery or slave trading in Pennsylvania (a 1780 state law would provide for the gradual emancipation of all slaves; slavery would not be legally abolished in America until two centuries after Penn, in 1865).

Despite its flaws, however, Penn's system was extremely democratic by the standards of his time. It would be unfair to judge Penn strictly by modern standards of democracy, for although he was an enlightened and progressive thinker, he remained a man of his own era.

William Penn was, indeed, something of a paradox. He devoted himself to the quest for religious liberation, yet his idea of liberty could stretch only far enough to include Christians; he would not allow atheists or Jews to vote or hold office in Pennsylvania. And although he denounced luxury and wrote earnest defenses of the simple, humble life, he furnished his homes handsomely, dined well, and never entirely abandoned a certain aristocratic gallantry and flair in his dress and manners. To the end of his days, he enjoyed associating with the learned and wellborn, and he continued to feel that, as proprietor of Pennsylvania, he

Thomas Birch's rendering of William Penn's arrival in America, The Landing of William Penn *(c. 1850).*

had certain rights above those of ordinary colonists.

Penn's sense of overlordship was reflected in his treatment of rents and taxes in Pennsylvania. When Penn acquired the grant to Pennsylvania, he offered to sell parcels of land in two sizes: 5,000 acres and 750 acres. The buyers would also have to pay a tax called a quitrent, due each year beginning in 1684 on every 100 acres of land. In Penn's eyes, these taxes were no different from the rents paid by the tenants of his Shanagarry estate in

Ireland—as a symbol of his position as proprietor, they went into his personal income. But many of the settlers disagreed. They maintained that the purpose of the quitrents should be to pay for administrative costs, used for projects such as erecting public buildings, maintaining roads, and the like.

When it became clear that the colonial government would have to levy new taxes to pay these public expenses, the settlers demanded that Penn pay them out of the quitrents. Penn refused, and the question of whether or not the colony was obligated to provide Penn with an income vexed relations between the settlers and their governor for years. Ultimately, Penn was disappointed that the Pennsylvania colony did not enrich his personal fortune as he had hoped it would. This is another example of Penn's complex motives: to him, Pennsylvania was both a "holy experiment" and a money-making business venture.

Immediately after he was granted the Pennsylvania charter by King Charles, Penn published several pamphlets describing the many virtues of the new colony. He wrote at length about Pennsylvania's geography, climate, wildlife and vegetation, and native peoples. This wealth of information was so impressive that Penn was elected to the Royal Society, England's most prestigious association of learned men. Later travelers would find, however, that not all of the information Penn published was accurate. Having not yet visited his new landholding, he had in fact compiled it from a variety of sources. But in 1682, not long after the death of his mother, he sailed to America. Guli was in poor health, so she stayed in England with the children. Penn embarked in August on a small ship appropriately called the *Welcome*.

The dismal crossing lasted about two months. Smallpox broke out aboard ship. Having survived the disease as a child, Penn was immune to it, so he was able to help nurse the sick. But many of the passengers died. He was greatly relieved to step ashore in America, not far from the mouth of the Delaware River. Thomas Birch, an early 18th-century American painter, captured this historic moment in a painting called *The Landing of William Penn*, which portrays a neatly dressed and wigged Quaker extending the hand of friendship to a tomahawk-bearing Indian on a wooded, deserted shore. (Like other images of Penn in America, however, this painting owes more to imagination than to fact. Penn came ashore briefly at the small settlement of New Castle, where some of the European settlers lived; however, no records exist of Indians being present.) He then went back aboard the *Welcome* and sailed upriver to the site of Philadelphia. From there, he issued a summons to all colonists to meet in March 1683 in Philadelphia to agree on the constitution he had prepared.

Before the assembly, Penn toured the neighboring colonies of New York and New Jersey. He also chose a site for his personal estate: a wooded plot of 8,400 acres, situated on a bend in the Delaware River 26 miles north of Philadelphia, not far from the present-day city of Trenton, New Jersey. As part of his plan to establish fair and equal relationships with the Native Americans who lived in his colony, Penn purchased the property from the local Leni-Lenape Indians rather than simply seizing it, as most European settlers would. He began working on plans for an estate that he would call Pennsbury Manor.

The March 1683 meeting of the colonists did not go as smoothly as Penn had expected. The Assembly demanded the right to create and debate bills. The Council asked why Penn was allotted three votes when everyone else had only one. And Penn was disappointed to discover that only about half of the colonists were Quakers and that not all of them agreed with his plans and rules. The governor and the colonists agreed to draw up a new constitution giving the Assembly the power to write its own bills—but only with the Council's permission. The new document also stated that the colony's proprietor did not have to pay the costs of operating the government, a point that would continue to

A view of the herb garden at Pennsbury Manor, Penn's personal estate. The garden was recreated when the manor was rebuilt in the 1940s.

draw debate for many years. In the end, no one was completely satisfied with the second constitution. Nevertheless, it was adopted in April 1683.

Penn faced another problem, concerning Pennsylvania's border with Maryland. He and Lord Baltimore, the proprietor of Maryland, disagreed over the boundary lines between their two colonies. The charters granted to each of them were in great conflict: Lord Baltimore claimed that his charter included Delaware and a portion of southern Pennsylvania that encompassed the site chosen for Philadelphia. They agreed to let the king decide the matter, but the dispute turned into a frustrating and drawn-out affair that would not be fully settled during Penn's lifetime.

While awaiting the king's decision, Penn made an extensive circuit of his colony, visiting the Native Ameri-

Benjamin West's painting, William Penn's Treaty with the Indians, *1771–72, is believed to be a symbolic representation of the event.*

can peoples living in the area. He was more respectful of their cultures than most Europeans of his time, making a point of paying for land the settlers occupied. As a result of Penn's overtures, relations between whites and Native Americans were more amicable in Pennsylvania than in any other American colony.

Legend says that Penn signed a treaty of friendship with the Delaware Indians at a place called Shackamaxon, just north of Philadelphia. This event is depicted in *William Penn's Treaty with the Indians*, a well-known painting by

Benjamin West, an 18th-century American painter who became popular in England. Although the painting includes probably the most familiar image of Penn, it cannot be regarded as a true portrait because it was painted in 1773, many years after Penn's death. The work also contains anachronisms, such as the inclusion of people who could not have been present in Shackamaxon in the 1680s wearing a style of clothing that had not yet been designed. Finally, the incident itself probably did not occur at the time and place suggested in the painting. Penn and the Delaware Indians did have a treaty, but the time and place of its signing are unknown. Nevertheless, West's painting exemplifies the reverence with which Americans still viewed William Penn nearly a century after he founded Pennsylvania.

Penn had hoped to make a long stay in his colony and to send for his family to join him. But in the summer of 1684 he was forced to return to London on urgent business. He not only wanted to press the king to settle the boundary dispute with Lord Baltimore, he was also worried about the very survival of his charter. Royal officials had caught several French ships trading with the American colonists. This was in violation of the colonial charters, which forbade the colonists to deal with any but British traders. A growing faction of the royal court insisted that the individual proprietors could not maintain sufficient control over their colonies and that all the charters should be withdrawn, placing British America fully under the control of the Crown. Penn hastened back to England to try to stop this threatening idea from gaining force. When he stepped aboard the vessel *Endeavour* for the homeward voyage, he did not suspect that it would be 15 years before he would see his colony again.

This engraving of William Penn holding the deed to his American land is typical of the way in which artists have portrayed the proprietor of Pennsylvania.

7

THE PROPRIETOR
OF PENN'S WOODS

THE YEARS FOLLOWING Penn's return to England were frequently sad and difficult. He encountered trouble and disappointment on four fronts: political events in England, differences of opinion with the Pennsylvania colonists, worsening financial troubles, and family problems.

To Penn's dismay, he learned that Quakers were being vigorously persecuted in England. He was himself fined or arrested several times for speaking at Quaker meetings. But although he protested to the king, Charles II was dying and had little time to worry about the treatment of the Nonconformists. When James, the duke of York, succeeded to the throne, he promised his old friend Penn that he would free the Quakers from jail and make life easier for all Nonconformists.

The duke was crowned King James II in February 1685, but he was unable to do as much for the Nonconformists as Penn had hoped. James was a Catholic ruler in a strongly anti-Catholic nation. Many of the king's subjects suspected that he was plotting to restore Catholic supremacy in England, and any toleration he showed for the Noncon-

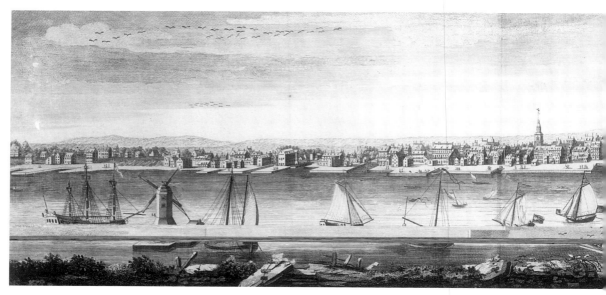

The "safe and commodious" harbor of Philadelphia, viewed from New Jersey across the Delaware River. By 1753, the date of this engraving, Philadelphia had grown into a thriving trade town of "near two thousand three hundred" residents, and was hailed for its spacious streets and protected location.

formists was viewed as paving the way for the rise of the Catholics. People reasoned that if the king allowed the Quakers and other Protestant Nonconformists to have rights, the Catholics might take advantage of them as well. And because William Penn worked tirelessly for religious freedom, old accusations that he was a secret Catholic were revived. Even some his of fellow Quakers in England and Pennsylvania began to believe these rumors, and they wished that Penn would distance himself from King James, for they, too, feared a Catholic return to power.

James remained on the throne for less than four years. In 1688, driven largely by the fear of Catholicism, the people and parliament of England demanded that he step down. Unlike the Civil War that had wracked the country a generation earlier, James's fall from power was bloodless. He quietly went into exile, and the throne of England was turned over to a Protestant European prince, William of Orange, and his wife, Mary, who was next in line to ascend the English throne.

William and Mary ushered in a new era of religious liberty with the Act of Toleration, which was passed in 1689.

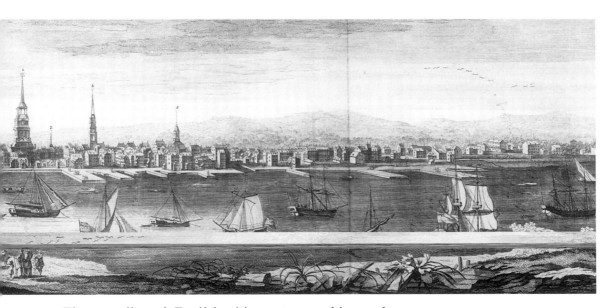

The act allowed English citizens to worship as they pleased without fear of punishment. Although some restrictions on holding public office still remained in force, the Act of Toleration was a milestone in the development of human rights and a model for similar laws in other countries. Much of the credit for its passing goes to William Penn, who had argued for more than 20 years that people whose beliefs placed them outside the state's established church did not automatically pose a threat to order and security and that these people deserved the same rights as everyone else. Penn himself was not well liked by King William and Queen Mary, however, mostly because he stubbornly refused to renounce his friendship with the exiled James, with whom he still corresponded. Indeed, Penn was kept under surveillance by royal agents until William and Mary decided that he was not a spy for James.

At the same time, Penn was struggling to maintain control of Pennsylvania. He had sent a succession of deputy governors to the colony, but none was effective and most were resented and mistrusted by the colonists. Even Penn's one success was not an easy victory: the royal court had upheld his claim against Lord Baltimore and had assigned the three counties on the border between the two colonies to Pennsylvania. However, disputes over the land continued. These counties remained rebellious for some time, and they occasionally threatened to withdraw from the colony.

Penn faced more serious problems with Pennsylvania as well. The Board of Trade and Plantations, a council that managed the affairs of the colonies under the control of the Crown, claimed that privately owned colonies such as Penn's were inefficient. The lords commissioners of the Board wanted to revoke, or cancel, the various charters and bring all colonies under their unified administration. In an attempt to avert this crisis, Penn proposed to the people of all the American colonies that they voluntarily form a union to cooperate in certain matters: to agree on a common currency, to control smuggling and other crimes, and if necessary, to prepare for their common defense against an attack by France or another hostile foreign power. In short, Penn's 1697 proposal, called *A Brief and Plain Scheme for Union*, was one of the earliest suggestions that the colonies unite and take on the responsibilities of self-government. And although he did not go so far as to suggest independence from England, Penn's notion of unity did foreshadow the concept of an American nation. But his call went unheard. Most colonists did not trust those in other colonies, and the idea of mutual cooperation was ignored.

The lords commissioners of trade and plantations were particularly angry about the amount of smuggling and illegal foreign trade that was going on in Pennsylvania (and in other colonies as well). In letter after letter, Penn urged the Council and the Assembly to enforce the trade laws, but the colonists did not take the matter seriously and nothing happened. Penn grew so frustrated that he threatened to revoke the constitution and rule the colony personally—another instance in which his belief in the ability of the

ordinary man to govern himself wisely collided with the unpalatable fact that people did not always do what he expected them to do.

Relations between Penn and the colony's other officials grew worse when war loomed between England and France. The French, who owned a large colony in Canada, had made allies among some Native American tribes, and England feared that a combined French and Indian force would attack the English colonies. (This did happen, but not until the middle of the 18th century.) Nearly every year, the Board of Trade and Plantations asked the colonies to contribute volunteers and funds for a militia, or armed force, to defend against possible attacks by the French or the Indians. Since the threat usually lay near the northern border of New York, far from Pennsylvania, the

William Penn and Hannah Callowhill are married in a Friends ceremony two years after the death of Penn's first wife, Guli. Penn and Hannah were survived by three sons, John, Thomas, and Richard.

The "Letitia House" in Philadelphia was the first brick building erected in the city. Penn gave the home to his daughter, Letitia.

Pennsylvanians felt little pressure to contribute. Furthermore, the Quaker population of the colony maintained that supporting a militia clashed with their principles of nonviolence, and they refused to contribute. But Penn's charter, like all of the colonial charters, required the colonists upon request of the Crown to contribute toward their own defense. The Board of Trade and Plantations seized upon Pennsylvania's refusal as evidence that the colony was badly managed.

The issue of defense greatly troubled the colony's proprietor. Penn was still a passionate believer in nonviolence. In 1693 he published an important book called *An Essay Toward the Present and Future Peace of Europe* that anticipated the establishment of the United Nations by two and one-half centuries. Penn called for an international parliament, where nations could settle their disputes without going to war. In this, as in so many other ideas, Penn was ahead of his time. But his proposal was disregarded. The problem of colonial defense did not go away, however, and Penn was forced to admit that under the charter he was responsible for enforcing the law. He was sometimes able to browbeat the reluctant colonists into paying the militia tax, but the amount fell short every year. To save his charter, Penn had to make up the difference out of his own pocket.

That pocket was no longer as deep as it had been. For Penn, Pennsylvania was a constant expense that brought no income; sales of land in Pennsylvania had tapered off, and the colonists balked at paying their quitrents. Furthermore, Ireland was once again wracked by uprisings and rebellions, which kept Penn from collecting his rents from Shanagarry.

Penn, who had grown up in a wealthy family and had never known poverty, sometimes displayed a casual attitude toward his own debts. He would acknowledge that he owed money to others, but he hated being asked to pay off his debts before he was ready. In the late 1680s, however, his creditors grew insistent. Among them was Philip Ford, Penn's former steward at Shanagarry who also had been his business manager for many years. Not only did Penn owe Ford an amount equal to several years' worth of his own salary, but he had also borrowed money from Ford. Now Ford pressed Penn for payment on these debts—with interest due. The amount came to nearly 4,300 pounds, a huge sum (by comparison, Penn sold 5,000-acre tracts in Pennsylvania for 100 pounds each).

Penn was gravely disappointed by Ford's lack of trust; he seemed unable to understand that Ford genuinely expected to receive the money. Finally, the two men agreed on a complicated system of mortgages that gave Penn an extended time to pay his debts and granted Ford a

A contemporary view of Pennsbury Manor. After Penn's death, the estate's main buildings fell into disrepair and by 1929 all of the original structures were gone. The manor house, outbuildings, and landscape were restored between 1933 and 1942, according to Penn's original instructions.

claim on the charter of Pennsylvania as security. Ford drew up the agreement, and Penn, never a prudent businessman, signed it without reading it—a rash act that caused serious problems a few years later.

The defense crisis came to a head in 1693. Penn's enemies on the Board of Trade and Plantations convinced King William that Pennsylvania's lack of a militia was a military danger. William suspended Penn's right to govern the colony and placed Pennsylvania under the command of New York. Penn's charter was restored in 1694, but only after the Pennsylvania Assembly passed a law that levied a militia tax.

Penn's personal life was filled with grief during these years. His dearly beloved wife, Gulielma Penn, died in

1694 at age 50, and after her death Penn himself was seriously ill for several months. His life took a positive turn two years later, when he married Hannah Callowhill, the daughter of a pious Quaker acquaintance. Although Hannah was 24 years younger than Penn, their marriage was happy. A shrewd and practical businesswoman, Hannah Penn helped her husband manage his increasingly tangled financial affairs. But Penn's joy in his new marriage was marred by the death of his elder son, Springett, just five weeks after the wedding.

Springett Penn, following in his father's footsteps, had been a devout Quaker. The same could not be said of Penn's surviving son, William Jr., who was called Billy. Impatient with Quaker plainness, Billy Penn ran up debts and made friends among a wild, loose-living set of young men. He married at age 17, and although Penn wanted him to take a hand in managing Pennsylvania, Billy refused to settle in what he thought was a wilderness. A few years later, in a curious echo of Penn's struggles with his own father, Billy was offered the captaincy of an Irish regiment. Penn proudly ordered him to turn it down; it was not good enough for a Penn, he declared.

Through all these years of trouble and turmoil, Penn yearned to return to Pennsylvania. At last, with his business affairs somewhat stable and his charter as secure as he could make it, he sailed for America in September 1699 with his new wife. In January 1700, two months after arriving in Pennsylvania, Hannah gave birth to a boy they named John—the first Penn born in Pennsylvania.

Penn was most eager to settle into Pennsbury Manor. The home had been built while he was in England, according to his detailed instructions—which called for large and beautiful gardens. But there was much work for him in the capital of Pennsylvania, whose population had grown to more than 5,000, second in size among American cities only to Boston, Massachusetts. Penn was saddened to see that Philadelphia's rapid growth had caused some of his precious schemes for parks and yards to be abandoned. Although broad boulevards and green areas remained, some districts of the city had become crowded and almost slumlike. His first priority, however, was strengthening the enforcement of the trade laws.

As he set about tidying up the disorder in Pennsylvania's administration, Penn learned that the colonists were as unhappy with his governorship as he was with them, and that the Council and the Assembly were divided into quarrelsome factions. This is common with governmental bodies, but the situation depressed Penn, who was growing weary of the constant struggle to impose his ideas. Together, he and the colonists developed a third constitution, which they called the Charter of Privileges. It eliminated the Council and created a larger Assembly, which became the sole lawmaking body of the colony. The new charter also granted the governor the power to veto acts passed by the Assembly. The only laws that were not changed were those that guaranteed religious liberty.

The Charter of Privileges created a balance of power in which the governor and the Assembly could act independently, but neither could compel the other to act against its will. The charter took effect in 1701 and continued in force until the American Revolution of the 1770s. It is thought to have contributed to the checks-and-balances system of the United States Constitution.

After April 1701, Penn and his family lived at Pennsbury. The mansion was furnished with elegant imported goods and staffed by numerous slaves and servants, leading many in the colony to remark that Penn lived richly for a simple Quaker. But Penn saw no contradiction between comfort and piety. As proprietor of the colony and a well-born individual, he felt entitled to a certain standard of living—and he was paying for it himself, after all. He hosted many splendid dinner parties in the paneled dining room at Pennsbury; among his guests were local Indian chiefs. Some of Penn's surviving letters show that he and Hannah sent to town for supplies such as bricks, lime, locks, and nails, and for provisions such as chocolate, flour, bacon, coffee, and corn meal. But like the Wanstead estate where Penn had grown up, Pennsbury was practically self-sufficient, with its own vineyard, orchard, farm, beehives, cemetery, bakery, brewery, and smokehouse for preserving meat. Located in a wild area far from other habitations and easily accessible only by water, the manor had to produce most of its own provisions. But Penn loved the solitude and natural beauty there. One of his favorite pastimes was walking in the garden, where he had cultivated rare plants imported from Europe and the West Indies. He also loved traveling to Philadelphia and back on the Delaware River in a large boat that he called his barge.

By the time the Charter of Privileges had been written, the Board of Trade and Plantations was threatening to revoke Penn's own charter to the Pennsylvania colony, so once more he went to London to do battle with the lords commissioners. He departed from Philadelphia in November 1701, intending to be away only a short time before settling for good in Pennsylvania. But he would never return. In two visits, Penn had spent a total of about four years in the colony he had created.

Penn's "greene countrie towne" of Philadelphia retains some of the broad, tree-lined avenues planned by its founder. The Benjamin Franklin Parkway, shown here, runs through Logan Circle, one of Penn's original five parks, and connects City Hall to the Philadelphia Museum of Art (upper left).

8

PENN'S LEGACY

AS WITH HIS earlier trip to London, Penn arrived to face a sea of troubles. One of the biggest issues concerned freedom of religion. There was a very real danger that the Act of Toleration would be revoked and that Nonconformists and Dissenters would again suffer fierce persecution. Some Friends even feared that Quakerism would be extinguished. Penn's life work, it seemed, might have been in vain.

The cause of all this worry was a princess named Anne, the younger sister of Queen Mary. Anne was a strict Anglican and strongly disapproved of Nonconformism. After she assumed the throne in March 1702, Penn wrote a letter telling the queen about the loyalty of "the people commonly called Quakers" and urging her to support the Act of Toleration. Whether she was moved by Penn's appeal or by more general considerations of policy, Anne responded graciously. "[Y]ou and your friends may be assured of my protection," she wrote to Penn, and she promised that the Act of Toleration would never be repealed.

Penn had less success in other areas. His son Billy had finally agreed to go to Pennsylvania and take up some administrative duties, but Billy proved careless and ineffective. Moreover, he made himself unpopular with the colonists by brawling in taverns, and he offended the pacifist Quakers by forming his own militia. Penn ordered him back to England in 1705, and Billy gave formal notice that he no longer considered himself a Quaker. Penn, who had spent a lifetime preaching the right of each individual to make his own religious decisions, had great difficulty accepting Billy's decision. His disappointment was reflected in his will, which left Billy the Irish estate but divided Pennsylvania among John, Thomas, and Richard, his three sons by Hannah.

Another problem for Penn was the matter of the money he owed to Philip Ford. When Ford died, his widow sued Penn for more than 11,000 pounds and threatened to claim ownership of Pennsylvania if he did not pay. The badly worded agreement Penn had signed with Ford a few years earlier gave his widow a disputable claim to the colony. Penn was forced to spend nine months in debtors' prison in 1707–08 for failing to pay the Ford family. He hired lawyers to sort out the mess, and finally the Fords agreed to accept 7,600 pounds as full payment. Penn raised the sum by borrowing from friends and by mortgaging lots in Pennsylvania.

Meanwhile, the Pennsylvania Assembly had grown lazy about collecting taxes and quitrents. The issue of defense money and militias also continued to cause trouble with the Board of Trade and Plantations. It seemed to Penn that the colonists argued with everything he tried to do. Profoundly frustrated, in 1703 he decided to wash his hands of the whole colony. He offered to sell back his charter to the lords commissioners for 40,000 pounds. However, the Board found the price—and the long list of privileges that Penn insisted on retaining—unacceptable, and the proposal went no further.

After the Ford claim was settled, Penn returned briefly to a life he loved. He spent part of 1709 and 1710 traveling through England, speaking at Quaker meetings, mak-

ing converts, and holding theological debates. In such activities, he found a calmness and certainty that he had never enjoyed as a colonial proprietor. Whatever his problems might be, as a missionary Penn was sure that he was doing God's will.

By now, however, the energy that had powered his life of service began to wane. Like his father, Penn suffered from gout, which often kept him bedridden for weeks at a time. He also endured several sharp attacks of something referred to as "fever," which may in fact have been minor strokes. In early 1710 he went home and gathered his family around him. He did little traveling thereafter.

Once again he tried to sell his charter back to Great Britain. Pennsylvania had become for Penn nothing more than a financial drain and a constant source of worry. The

William Penn and many of his family members, including his wives, are buried in the graveyard of Jordans Meeting House in Buckinghamshire, England.

"holy experiment" had not turned out quite as he had planned, and he was willing to separate himself from it and leave the colonists to work out their own destiny. After renewing negotiations with the queen's representatives, he agreed in 1712 to accept 12,000 pounds for Pennsylvania. But before the contract could be completed, Penn suffered a severe stroke that left him confused and partially paralyzed. Because he was unable to conduct business, the sale was postponed.

Penn never regained enough strength or mental powers to complete the agreement. He remained the proprietor of Pennsylvania in name, and Hannah Penn took over the correspondence and other duties involved in long-distance administration. Although she proved a capable manager, the Pennsylvania Assembly had achieved a fairly high degree of independence, and most of the time it simply made its own decisions. The Penn family's ownership of the colony was increasingly regarded as a courtesy rather than a controlling factor in Pennsylvania's government.

Penn grew weaker and more confused as the years passed. Hannah tended to him affectionately, but he had entered a long, gentle decline. For some time, he was unable to recognize old friends, to attend Quaker meetings, or to debate any of the philosophical issues to which he had devoted so many years of his life. He died on July 30, 1718, and was buried in the Quaker cemetery in Jordans, Buckinghamshire, in England.

Penn's son Billy died two years after his father; Hannah Penn died in 1726. Penn's descendants retained the official proprietorship of Pennsylvania until the American Revolution nullified all colonial charters with Great Britain.

Penn's legacy lives on in Pennsylvania, which is still called the Quaker State. The Quaker heritage is felt especially in the Philadelphia area, where many Friends have become prominent in business and politics and where Friends schools are among the city's finest. Pennsbury Manor, which fell into ruin after the Penns died, has been

A watercolor by American artist N. C. Wyeth depicts the dreams and accomplishments of Pennsylvania's founder.

restored to its original state and now serves as a Penn museum. Vestiges of the "greene countrie towne" that Penn planned are still evident in Philadelphia, which has one of the country's largest urban park systems. Atop Philadelphia's city hall stands a 37-foot-tall bronze statue of the state's founder, cast in 1893 by the sculptor Alexander Milne Calder. The figure, holding a charter in one hand, gazes broodingly down on the City of Brotherly Love, whose residents treat "Billy Penn" with familiar affection. (While the building underwent extensive renovations in the 1980s, citizens passed out "Free Billy Penn" buttons to alert others that the statue had been imprisoned for too long by scaffolding; and Penn's likeness is often dressed in jerseys or hats featuring the logos of local professional sports teams that are bound for playoff games.)

Penn also exerted a powerful influence on the formation of the United States. At a time when few thinkers ventured to discuss religious liberty, government by representation, and respect for individual freedom, Penn gave voice to these and other liberal concepts that came to be seen as distinctively American values. Thomas Jefferson, one of America's founding fathers, called Penn "the greatest lawgiver the world has produced."

Penn's decent treatment of Native Americans also set an example—one that was not, unfortunately, followed in many other areas of the country. And Penn encouraged a greater degree of ethnic and cultural diversity than any other colony in America could claim.

But Penn's most important legacy reaches far beyond the founding of Pennsylvania: his commitment to the rights of conscience—the right of the individual to choose his own faith, to refrain from making war, and to preach and write freely. Penn was not completely free of prejudices, nor did he always manage to follow his own principles without compromise. But he made a conscious, daily effort to live the best life he could, hoping to inspire others to do likewise.

Penn was a singularly enlightened and compassionate man, not only for his own time, but for all times. In 1693 he summed up his beliefs in this way: "Love is above all; and when it prevails in us all, we shall all be Lovely and in Love with God and with one another."

The 37-foot-tall bronze sculpture of William Penn, created by the sculptor Alexander Milne Calder, stands outside City Hall before being raised atop its tower. The building was completed in 1901.

APPENDIX

PENN'S LEGACY OF RELIGIOUS FREEDOM: PHILADELPHIA HISTORIC SITES

Arch Street Friends Meeting House, the oldest meeting house in Philadelphia and the largest in the world. 320 Arch Street, Philadelphia PA. 215-627-2667.

Christ Church, built 1727–1754 and containing the "600-year-old font" from England in which Penn was baptized. Second and Market Streets, Philadelphia PA. 215-922-1695.

City Hall, topped by Alexander Milne Calder's bronze sculpture of William Penn; the statue faces northeast toward Penn Treaty Park, the site where Penn is said to have negotiated his final agreement with the local Native Americans. Penn Square, at intersection of Broad and Market Streets, Philadelphia PA.

Congregation Mikveh Israel, one of the oldest Jewish congregations in the United States. 44 North 4th Street, Philadelphia PA. 215-922-5446. http://www.libertynet.org/~kkmi

Free Quaker Meeting House, founded in 1783 by Quakers who were "read out of meeting" for assisting in the American Revolution. Arch Street between 5th and 6th Streets, Philadelphia PA.

Historic St. George's United Methodist Church, called the "cradle of American Methodism," the world's oldest Methodist church in continuous service. 235 North 4th Street, Philadelphia PA. 215-925-7788.

Mother Bethel African Methodist Episcopal Church, founded by Richard Allen, the second oldest black congregation in the country, situated on the oldest parcel of real estate continuously owned by African Americans. 419 Richard Allen Avenue (Lombard Street between 5th and 6th Streets), Philadelphia PA. 215-925-0616.

Old First Reformed Church, one of the earliest German Reformed Churches in America. The charter under which the church operates was granted by William Penn's sons Thomas and Richard. 4th and Race Streets, Philadelphia PA. 215-922-4566.

Old Pine Street Presbyterian Church, called the "Church of the Patriots." The land on which it stands was purchased from William Penn's sons Thomas and Richard. 412 Pine Street, Philadelphia PA. 215-925-8051. http://www.libertynet.org/~oldpine/

Old St. Augustine's Church, once home to the "sister" of the Liberty Bell (a replacement bell ordered when the original cracked), which was destroyed by fire during the 1840s. 4th and New Streets, Philadelphia PA. 215-627-3911.

Old St. Joseph's Church, founded in 1733; the oldest Roman Catholic Church in Philadelphia. 321 Willings Alley, Philadelphia, PA. 215-923-1733. http://www.sju.edu/~osj/

Old St. Mary's Church, Philadelphia's first Roman Catholic cathedral, site of the first public religious commemoration of the Declaration of Independence. 252 South 4th Street, Philadelphia PA. 215-923-7930.

Pennsbury Manor, the Pennsylvania home of William Penn. 400 Pennsbury Memorial Road, Morrisville, PA. 215-946-0400. http://www.libertynet.org/~pensbury

Penn's Landing, encompassing the spot where William Penn first touched ground; today a riverside park and summer concert venue. Columbus Avenue (formerly Delaware

Avenue) between South and Vine Streets, Philadelphia, PA.

St. Peter's Church, built by the Church of England, completed in 1761. 313 Pine Street, Philadelphia, PA. 215-925-5968.

Society Hill, named for the Free Society of Traders, a stock company to whom William Penn granted land and privileges. Extending from 2nd to 5th Street and from Walnut to Lombard Streets, Philadelphia, PA.

Washington Square, one of the five original squares laid out in William Penn's plan for the "green country towne"; originally called Southeast Square (Quakers did not believe in naming places after people); on its edge was the site of the Orange Street Friends' Meeting House. Bounded by 6th and 7th Streets and by Walnut and South Seventh Street, Philadelphia, PA.

Welcome Park, the only site in historic Philadelphia dedicated to the life and contributions of William Penn; contains a marble replica of Penn's original city plan and a small copy of the William Penn sculpture atop City Hall. William Penn's son, John, was born on this site. Second Street and Sansom Street Alley, Philadelphia, PA.

Wyck House, one of the oldest surviving buildings in the Philadelphia area, owned and lived in by nine generations of one Quaker family. 6026 Germantown Avenue, Philadelphia, PA. 215-848-1690. http://pobox.upenn.edu/~converse/

OTHER LINKS:

History of Manayunk, PA (land granted by Penn):
http://www.gim.net/gic/north_america/usa/pennsylvania/philadelphia/manayunk/history/

Pennsylvania Dutch Country Welcome Center (Lancaster County, PA):
http://www.800padutch.com/

Quaker Resources: http://www.quaker.org/

Religious Tolerance: http://www.religioustolerance.org/

FURTHER READING

Bronner, Edwin B. *William Penn's Holy Experiment: The Founding of Philadelphia, 1681–1701*. Philadelphia: Temple University Press, 1962.

————. *William Penn, 17th Century Founding Father: Selections from His Political Writings*. Wallingford, Pa.: Pendle Hill, 1975.

Buranelli, Vincent. *The King and the Quaker: A Study of William Penn and James II*. Philadelphia: University of Pennsylvania Press, 1962.

Burt, Struthers. *Philadelphia: Holy Experiment*. Garden City, N.Y.: Doubleday, 1945.

Dunn, Mary Maples. *William Penn: Politics and Conscience*. Princeton, N.J.: Princeton University Press, 1967.

Fantel, Hans. *William Penn: Apostle of Dissent*. New York: Morrow, 1974.

Foster, Genevieve. *The World of William Penn*. New York: Scribners, 1973.

Fradin, Dennis B. *The Pennsylvania Colony*. Chicago: Children's Press, 1988.

Gray, Elizabeth J. *Penn*. New York: Viking, 1938.

Illick, Joseph. *William Penn the Politician: His Relations with the English Government*. Ithaca, N.Y.: Cornell University Press, 1967.

Soderland, Jean, ed. *William Penn and the Founding of Pennsylvania: A Documentary History*. Philadelphia: University of Pennsylvania Press and Historical Society of Pennsylvania, 1983.

Stevens, S. K. *The Pennsylvania Colony*. London: Collier-Macmillan, 1970.

Tolles, Frederick, and Gordon Alderfer, eds. *The Witness of William Penn*. New York: Macmillan, 1957.

Trussell, John B., Jr. *William Penn: Architect of a Nation*. Harrisburg, Pa.: Pennsylvania Historical and Museum Commission, 1980.

Wildes, Harry Emerson. *William Penn*. New York: Macmillan, 1974.

CHRONOLOGY

1642–51   English Civil War pits Royalists against Parliamentarians

1644   William Penn born on October 14 in London, England

1649   King Charles I executed by Parliamentarians;
England declared a commonwealth

1653   Oliver Cromwell named Lord Protector of the Commonwealth

1658   Cromwell dies; his son, Richard, succeeds him

1660   English monarchy restored when Charles II assumes British throne
William Penn attends college in Oxford but leaves during his second year

1662–64   Penn travels and studies in France and travels to Italy with Robert Spencer

1665   Penn serves briefly in the Royal Navy
London is ravaged by an outbreak of bubonic plague

1666   The Great Fire sweeps through London, destroying 80 percent of the city
Penn goes to Ireland to manage family property

1667   Penn joins the Friends of Truth (Quakers) and is jailed for attending a Quaker
meeting in Cork

1668   Penn is imprisoned in the Tower of London for treason following the publication of his religious pamphlet *Sandy Foundations Shaken*

1669   Penn writes *No Cross, No Crown* about Quaker and Puritan beliefs

1670   Penn is arrested for preaching in the street and acquitted after a landmark controversial trial

1671   While in jail again for refusing to swear an oath, Penn writes *The Great Case
of Liberty of Conscience* about religious toleration; after his release from
prison, Penn travels through the Netherlands and Germany seeking converts to
Quakerism

1672   Penn marries Gulielma Springett

1674   Penn becomes involved with a Quaker colony in New Jersey

1677   Penn and other Quakers travel to the Netherlands, Belgium, and Germany on a
missionary tour

1681	Charles II grants the large American colony of Pennsylvania to Penn
1682	Penn travels to Pennsylvania to preside over first assembly of the "holy experiment"
1684	Penn returns to England to negotiate the Maryland-Pennsylvania boundary with the king
1685	James II, brother of Charles II, becomes king
1688	James II is deposed; William of Orange and his wife, Mary, become joint sovereigns
1689	The Act of Toleration is passed in England, broadening religious liberty
1693	Penn writes *An Essay Toward the Present and Future Peace of Europe*, calling for an international parliament
1693–94	Penn falls out of favor with the court and temporarily loses title to the Pennsylvania colony
1694	Penn's wife, Gulielma, dies
1696	Penn marries Hannah Callowhill
1699	Penn returns to America to head the Pennsylvania colony
1700	Penn and his family move to Pennsbury Manor, outside of Philadelphia
1701	A constitution called the *Charter of Privileges* becomes law in Pennsylvania; Penn leaves the colony for England
1702	Anne, daughter of James II, assumes the British throne
1703	Penn attempts to sell the Pennsylvania colony to the British government
1712	Penn makes a deal with the British government and begins preparations to sell Pennsylvania, but he suffers a stroke and the sale is postponed, never to be completed
1718	After several years as an invalid, Penn dies on July 30 and is buried in Buckinghamshire, England

INDEX

Act of Toleration, 86–87, 97
Amyraut, Moïse, 43, 55, 61
Anne (queen of England), 97
Anglican Church. *See* Church of England
Anglo-Dutch Wars, 44, 45, 47–48

Billinge, Edward, 68, 69
Birch, Thomas, 80
Board of Trade and Plantations, 88, 90, 92, 95, 98
Brief and Plain Scheme for Union, A, 88
Bushell, Edward, 64–66

Calder, Alexander Milne, 102
Charles I (king of England), 20, 22, 25, 37
Charles II (king of England), 12, 25, 31, 32, 33, 35, 37, 38–39, 44, 47–48, 62, 72, 73, 79, 85
Chigwell Free Grammar School, 28–29
Christ Church College, 36, 41
Church of England, 21, 22, 28, 29, 38, 43, 53, 55, 61, 62, 73
Civil War, English, 20–26, 86
Coale, Josiah, 56, 59, 72
Congreve, William, 37
Cooke, Francis, 61
Cromwell, Oliver, 22,

25–26, 30–31, 32, 35

Dissenters, 21, 52, 62, 97

England, 11, 19, 21, 25, 26, 37, 44, 52, 63, 64, 65, 67, 68, 71, 72, 79, 85, 88, 98
Essay Toward the Present and Future Peace of Europe, An, 90–91

Fenwick, John, 68
Fifth Monarchists, the, 16, 52
Ford, Philip, 63, 91–92, 98
Foundation of God Standeth, The (Vincent), 61
Fox, George, 52, 53, 57, 59, 66, 67–68, 72

Great Case of Liberty of Conscience, The, 66

"Hat honor," 42–43, 52

Inner Light doctrine, 32, 52
Innocency with Its Open Face, 62
Inns of Court, 45
Ireland, 11, 12, 14, 16, 17, 21, 22, 23, 24, 25, 26, 31, 35, 49, 50, 51, 55, 63, 79, 91

James II (king of England), 39, 47, 49, 63, 72, 85, 87
Jefferson, Thomas, 102

Jenkins, Leoline, 72, 73

Lincoln's Inn, 45, 48
Loe, Thomas, 32, 51, 57, 59, 66
London, England, 22, 23, 26, 27, 31, 32, 35, 38, 40, 41, 44, 45, 47, 56, 57, 61, 63, 64, 95, 97
Great Fire of, 48–49
Great Plague of, 48, 49, 76

Louis XIV (king of France), 42, 44

Markham, William, 74
Mead, William, 63–66, 76
More, Thomas, 74

Native Americans, 73, 74, 80, 81–83, 89, 94, 102
Naylor, James, 55
No Cross, No Crown, 62
Nonconformists, 21, 32, 28, 49, 52, 55, 85, 86, 97

Oxford University, 36–41, 42, 44, 45
Owen, John, 38, 39–40, 41, 43, 55, 61

Penn, Gulielma Springett "Guli" (first wife), 28, 59–60, 62, 63, 67, 68, 79, 92–93
Penn, Hannah Callowhill (second wife), 93, 94, 100

PICTURE CREDITS

Rebecca Stefoff is a freelance writer of biographies and other nonfiction works for young readers, including *Women Pioneers* (1996) and *Finding the Lost Cities* (1997). She has also served as the editorial director of Chelsea House's PLACES AND PEOPLES OF THE WORLD and LET'S DISCOVER CANADA series. A resident of Philadelphia for 19 years, she now lives in Portland, Oregon.

James Scott Brady serves on the board of trustees with the Center to Prevent Handgun Violence and is the Vice Chairman of the Brain Injury Foundation. Mr. Brady served as Assistant to the President and White House Press Secretary under President Ronald Reagan. He was severely injured in an assassination attempt on the president, but remained the White House Press Secretary until the end of the administration. Since leaving the White House, Mr. Brady has lobbied for stronger gun laws. In November 1993, President Bill Clinton signed the Brady Bill, a national law requiring a waiting period on handgun purchases and a background check on buyers.

THE
SEVEN
NUMBERS

THAT WILL SAVE YOUR LIFE

SCOTT CONARD, MD, DABFM, FAAFP

THE SEVEN NUMBERS

THAT WILL SAVE YOUR LIFE

2nd Edition: The Corporate Edition

www.thesevennumbers.com

DEDICATION

This book is dedicated to Pat Dunn, a dear friend and visionary who has clung tightly to his vision of great healthcare and long life for every person. We have been through much together in our quest to find ways to inform and support people who are ready to live long and vital lives. He won the Healthcare Hero award for the Dallas Business Journal in 2008 for his innovation and ingenuity in healthcare. He will always be an inspiration, an admired colleague and a dear friend.

NOTE FROM DR. SCOTT CONARD:

In this the Third Edition, the Corporate Edition we see how getting the Seven Numbers to goal is saving corporations like Hilti millions of dollars in health care costs. By addressing these numbers they are getting Metabolic Syndrome under control and *adding years to the life and life to the years of their employees.*

Converging Health, LLC (www.ConvergingHealth.com) has created the data analytics and services (the MyPHA Program) to insure theat every employee and their family members have the best change to get their Seven Numbers to goal and a Personal Health Assistant (PHA) who guides them effectively through the healthcare system. The result? Healthier employees, lower cost, and cultural transformation with appreciative, empowered, effictive employees in action at work and at home.

contents
THE SEVEN NUMBERS

foreword

THE SEVEN NUMBERS

We are at a unique moment in time. Finally the incentives for individuals and corporations to maintain or improve their health are aligning. Health insurance policies now create incentives for employees to engage in their health – either positive incentives with rewards for getting screening and other appropriate exams done, or negative incentives by having the employee at risk for the health care costs, sometimes up to $2000 or $3000. In contrast to previous years where low copays and deductibles lead to complacency and, as long as employees felt fine, the tendency to avoid going to the doctor, today acting earlier, regardless of how one feels to catch problems early or prevent problems makes both health and financial sense.

Corporations are beginning to act to insure early engagement occurs. At Converging Health, LLC we serve over 250,000 members with clinical health risk determination, proactive concierge engagement, and population health. Consistently we see that a small number of employees, six to eight percent, account for 65 - 80% of the money spent on health care each year. An additional 10 - 20% spend no money on healthcare each year, and of great concern, it is not uncommon to find that 40% of men a corporations, without incentives or penalties to engage, have not gone to a Primary care doctor in over 2 years - meaning that their national screening, preventive visits, and chronic care guidlines are not being followed over 30 - 40% of the time. As the Institute of Medicine has pointed out "we know what to do, but are not doing what we know!"

What are the consequences of this way of managing our health? *Employees are being diagnosed with advanced disease.* By the time it is uncovered, it costs literally millions, if not billions, of dollars to fight. People suffer, they miss work, they often end up disabled or die, and their families and employers lose a valuable member of their team.

This doesn't have to happen. At Converging Health we find that 60 – 75% of these catastrophic costs are usually due to one of four conditions; 1. Cardiovascular disease (strokes or heart disease), 2. Cancer, 3. Musculoskeletal disease (joint or spine problems), or 4. Diabetes. This may be very good news. At least three of these conditions could have been prevented or delayed – and the fourth with early recognition significantly improved. The problem is we are acting too late, not that we could not have acted.

How could we reverse the tide of disease? Consider the natural progression of these diseases:

* Stage 0 is when you have a risk of getting a condition, but there is no sign of it in your body. Examples are when you have a strong family history of cancer, heart disease or diabetes,
* Stage 1 disease is when you have begun to increase your risk of disease. Commonly this is a lack of training (the First Number) and an increase in abdominal girth and weight (the Second Number) leading to a lack of fitness, overweight and obesity which increases the risks of all four diseases,

6

- Stage 2 disease means that things are starting to progress and you are headed straight into TROUBLE! For both diabetes and heart disease this is when metabolic syndrome develops. For musculoskeletal conditions this is when strains and sprains begin to appear,

- At Stage 3 you have developed the disease and the timer on developing significant consequences has begun. Diabetes, heart disease (although you still have not had a heart attack) or blocked arteries in your neck, head, aorta or legs are now present. For musculoskeletal disease this is when chronic pain begins and a nerve is being pinched or stimulated, and

- Stage 4 disease means that you are dealing with significant consequences of the disease. This is blindness, amputations or kidney failure for people with diabetes; heart attacks or failure, strokes, and/or aneurysms for people with cardiovascular disease; and surgery for those with musculoskeletal disease – which may or may not help the issue.

Cancer is somewhat different. For most cancers during stage 1 and 2 disease the tumor is still in only one place making the possibility of curing the disease over 50% - and in some cases 80 – 98%. In stage three the cancer has spread to tissues in the local area and the chance of surviving drops significantly. Finally in stage four the cancer has spread to other parts of the body making the chance of survival much lower and requiring more dramatic therapy. So just as in the other conditions the time to identify and reverse the disease is in stage one, or at latest stage two when a cure is much more likely.

What do all four of these conditions have in common? In stage 0 – 2 if you ask a person how they are feeling there is a good chance they will say **"I feel fine."** How does weight gain, decreasing fitness, metabolic syndrome or stage one or two cancer feel? Surprisingly they don't hurt. There may be some fatigue or lethargy relative to when they had stage 0 disease, but usually there are few or no symptoms. Examples of this are;

- Hypertension (the great silent killer),
- Diabetes - over a third of people with diabetes do not even know they have it,
- Heart disease - according to the American Heart Association, over two thirds of women and one half of men die the first time they have a symptom (chest pain, stage 4 disease) and,
- Musculoskeletal disease - over 50% of people who have significant changes on their x-rays consistent with degeneration of joints or their spine but have no symptoms.

If you think about it this is a good thing for our productivity (in the short run) – our bodies allow us to function without pain as long as possible, until the disease has reached a critical stage, and then we feel symptoms.

But this has contributed to our current health care crisis. *People engage in their health when they feel bad – and it is often, if not usually, too late.* So the question of the day is; how do we get employees who "feel fine" to become active and engaged in their health? How do we insure that they know their risk and can act to eliminate or reduce their risk of disease?

Hilti North America has figured it out. Karen Rogers and Cary Evert began a journey to insure that every Teammate at Hilti knew their numbers with biometric screening. If they had metabolic syndrome they gave them a program to reduce or eliminate their risk (Naturally Slim or Weight Watchers), and Hilti brought in a cafeteria vendor who provides flavorful and much healthier alternatives (Guckenheimer) – and diabetes and heart disease dropped from the #1 and #3 categories of spend down to the #5 and #7 categories.

Cancer emerged as the next challenge, and we worked to create the early version of the Personal Health Assistant Program to support Teammates getting their age and gender appropriate screening done – and 39% more pre-cancer and cancer was identified earlier and treatment was performed at 25% of the cost from previous years (pre-cancer and stage 1 cancer is much less expen- sive to treat). Finally, their total health care spend has been significantly less than their peers, actually dipping into a negative spend at times over the past few years.

The future of healthcare has arrived. The paradigm is changing. Corporations are real-izing that they must insure that employees know and act on their Seven Numbers if they begin to move out of range. They are creating incentives to align and activate employees. Soon mechanisms for doctors and the healthcare system to increase health, as opposed to treating (or creating) disease will align and the health of our nation will take a signifi-cant leap forward. The "I feel fine" syndrome with be replaced with the "I manage my numbers" state of health and well-being.

If you are a leader in a corporation join the Stage O Movement. By providing empowering programs and benefit design, you have the power to support every employee and their family to know and manage their Seven Numbers. Who knows, depending on the size of your company you may save more lives than most fam-ily doctors dreamed of in their careers! Declare "not on my shift" and stop our true enemy – *disease* in its tracks.

Scott Conard, MD

foreword

Greg Massey
CEO, First United Bank

At First United, we strive to inspire and empower others to Spend Life Wisely. Health and Wellness is one of the four pillars of Spend Life Wisely. When we feel our best, both mentally and physically, we are better able to focus on the things that matter most in our lives.

I can testify to what taking care of yourself can do to improve your life, both personally and professionally. When I got serious about my health several years ago, I saw a huge positive change in my energy level, alertness, mindset, and my medical numbers. Devoting time to taking care of myself has allowed me to take better care of the people I love the most – my family, friends, employees and my community.

During my health journey I turned to my good friend, and author of this book, Dr. Scott Conard. Scott is passionate about helping others transform their lives. Knowing Scott's passion, I trusted that he could help me focus on what matters most.

For me and First United, Health and Wellness is all about maintaining a healthy diet, exercising regularly, resting, and reducing stress whenever possible. I trust that this book will be a guide to help you do just that!

Greg Massey
CEO, First United Bank

foreword

Cary R. Evert, President and CEO, Hilti North America

Just over four years ago we were having a medical benefits meeting at Hilti. Our costs were going up rapidly and difficult economic times created a very real challenge to our company. Our advisors were recommending that we change directions and become more proactive and aggressive with our health benefits by doing biometric testing and taking other steps that would mean more cost and a change in our culture towards wellness. The decision we made was to bet on the future health of our team members and not short measures to control cost.

That was the beginning of our journey on how we deal with medical care and investment in our people and today I am very proud of what we have accomplished with our team. First we began to check the numbers with biometric testing and then various programs which greatly lowered certain medical risks for those who participated. We also began to change our culture – going "smoke free", challenging team members to get active, and improving the health benefits of the food served in our campus restaurant.

We are beginning to win the Game of Health:

- First with *awareness* by getting the numbers with biometrics and an expanded panel of tests this year (we did this because we discovered that a high percentage of our team-mates were not going to doctors regularly so we did expanded blood work).

- Then *education* to understand team members gaps in care and to make sure they get what they need to have done when they need it,

- Helping our team members *overcome their habits* with no co-insurance for wellness visits, and offering healthy food in our restaurant,

- Increasing appropriate *accountability*—if you care for yourself, then we will care for you; if you don't then you are penalized for not showing self-responsibility, and

- *Sharing and celebrating* our successes with you.

Our team members have been incredibly successful;

- Our metabolic syndrome rates (pre-diabetes and pre-heart disease) have gone down significantly.

- We are finding cancers earlier - in stage 1 and 2, not 3 or 4.

- Our teammates are not as sick, they are not having as many catastrophic problems, and thus they do not need to go to the hospital or to the doctor as much. Costs are going down for the right reason; we are getting healthier.

- Engagement and commitment is going up as more and more team members are participating in our efforts.
- Our "catastrophic" medical events have gone down.
- And our business results are growing beyond our expectations!

Had we not changed directions on medical issues a few years ago, I believe we would have had more heart attacks, strokes, diabetes and other problems. The participation of our team members is making a significant difference.

But that is not all, we are not done. We are looking to the future. What else can we do for and with our team members? We are open to what works. We are committed to finding empowering motivating programs for our team.

We have positive momentum around our programs.

- We believe that having a strong sense of community purpose is important so we are giving our teammates 2 days of community service.
- We want to identify and encourage our teammates to be able to find great primary care and specialist doctors. We are going to help find and identify these to support our team members. We want our team to get what they need when they need it.
- We want to help people when they do have a significant event navigate the system and be successful despite their challenges.
- Our team members are being more proactive with their providers. Problems are being discovered and more invested in their care. We are setting the bar and we expect our service levels to be met. As we begin to think this way, we learn what to ask for, and we are getting better and better care.

But our success doesn't stop there. Recently our team members voted us the #1 company in the US to sell for. One of the rankings on this survey is healthcare, and we scored 8 of 10 in this category. That is no accident. The performance of this company is based upon highly energetic, motivated teammates serving our customers every day. We can't do that if they we are ill or in poor health. We can't do this if our teammates have advanced cancer, silent heart disease, or uncontrolled diabetes.

This book is a great place to get started. Simple concepts in easy to understand language is what we all need to navigate the complexity of the medical industry. If you read this book, you also can start your journey towards a happy, healthy life for you and your team. Good Luck!!!

Cary R. Evert
President and Chief Executive Officer
Hilti North America

foreword

Randall Boyd,
CEO Guckemheimer, Inc.

A perfect storm is raging across corporate America. Out of control health care costs are requiring our employees to contribute more and more of their paychecks while employers face double digit increases in their share of the cost for employee health care. Meanwhile, our country continues to lose the fight against obesity that not only affects our nation's workers but their children as well. Ultimately, it's a threat to our country's competitiveness on the global stage.

Dr. Scott Conard made a decision that the best place to attack these issues through a partnership with corporate leaders to educate employees about their health at work. He became increasingly frustrated with his inability to affect patient outcomes as a primary care physician that saw his patients only twice a year. He knew that employers were very interested in improving employee health and he has now committed his career to that effort. This book is about PREVENTION. Prevention is the best way to reduce health care costs and prevent obesity.

We have learned about "Metabolic Syndrome" from Dr. Conard. And, one of our clients who has actually reduced their corporate health care costs and saved many employee's lives through a program of metabolic syndrome prevention. That program includes screening, nutrition, and exercise. Everyone wins with this program. Employees avoid catastrophic health problems by identifying and eliminating the risk factors while reducing their health care costs. Employers win by having healthier and more productive employees that require a lower investment in health insurance. Families win by learning about healthy lifestyles from the knowledge their family member has learned at work.

I'm convinced this is a big part of the solution we so desperately need in our country to overcome the health care crisis. Our company provides delicious healthy food to corporations. We think we can be a partner in this solution. We would love to hear what you think about this book and welcome the opportunity to share more of what we have learned.

Randall Boyd
CEO Guckenheimer, Inc.
Redwood Shores, California

Karen Rogers, Wellness Consultant

When I started my career in the insurance industry, I never expected to be saving lives. Yet, 22 years later, as I consult employers on their employee benefits strategy, it is what I do.

The term "wellness program" has become stale and benign as employers look to "check the box". However, more than ever before, employers have a unique opportunity today to make a life-saving difference. Employers can and should influence employees and their families to live a healthy, full, and ultimately, productive life. And, company culture does not have to suffer. Rather, it can thrive in this environment, where employees know that their company and senior leadership are looking out especially for them.

What does it take and how do you do it? There are several keys to success in developing and delivering the right health program:

- *Commitment to the long term:* You are not going to change life-long behaviors over-night, nor will you convince your employees in one communication that you are doing what is best for them

- *Every population is the same and is different:* In other words, know your population – their health risks, their health behaviors, their communication preferences, what motivates them. Many of these are the same across employers, but you must build the program that works for your company and your employees

- *Be creative:* Some of this is unchartered territory. Be willing to try new ideas and build what works for you

- *Measure and share results:* HR and Senior leadership are not the only ones who are interested and need to know if you are making progress – share it with your employ-ees. Shout it from the rooftop – you are saving lives and making a difference

- *Walk the walk:* Senior leadership must be on board with the commitment and investment of the company; and messages of support must start from the top

When developed for the right reasons and with the right goals in mind, employers can realize: An improvement in employee loyalty and engagement in the success of the company; a healthier, more productive population; and lower costs over time.

As I review the latest results of one of the most successful programs I've been privileged to help develop, I am struck by the results and the impact that we are making every day, savings lives of the employees and their families we serve. I urge you to consider how your company can save lives, too.

Karen Rogers
Wellness Consultant and Vice President – Business Development
Holmes Murphy & Associates

SECTION**ONE**

GETTING STARTED

IT'S AS SIMPLE AS A, B, C

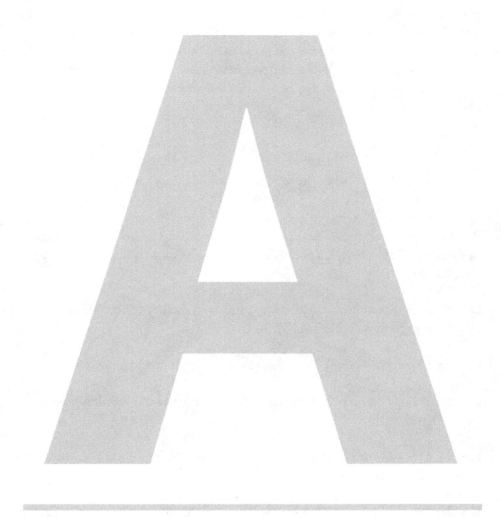

UNDERSTANDING
THE SEVEN NUMBERS

The first part of any trip is realizing where you are and deciding where you want to go. Likewise, achieving health and fitness starts with assessing where you are now and where you want to be in the days ahead. To do this, I took the word TROUBLE and developed an acronym that stands for seven primary areas of importance connected with our physical health. In the word TROUBLE…

....

T is for *Training*: It shows the amount of activity in your life as reflected in your level of fitness.

R is for *Roundness*: It can be captured by your waist circumference or your Body Mass Index (BMI), a formula comparing your weight in relation to your height.

O is for *Oil*: It is a measure of the quantity and quality of the fats in your blood (triglycerides, LDL, HDL).

U is for *Unacceptable Sugar*: It indicates the sugar levels in your blood.

B is for *Blood Pressure*: It measures the pressure on the inside of your blood vessels.

L is for *Lousy Habits*: It identifies things in your life that hold you back from good health.

E is for *Exploding Plaque*: It exposes the fat buildup inside your arteries that leads to cardiovascular disease (heart attacks and strokes), the #1 killer in the U.S. for both women and men.

....

By assessing your TROUBLE numbers, you can accurately determine where you are in the spectrum of good health—healthy, borderline, or unhealthy. Let me explain with these three diagrams.

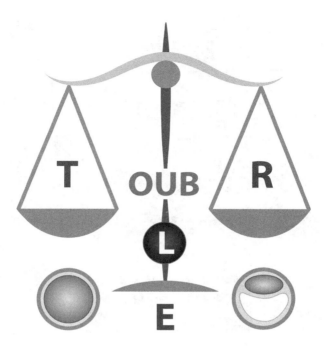

What is shown in this first diagram is that the balance between training (**T**) and roundness (**R**) manifests in our body in how much oil (**O**) and unacceptable sugar (**U**) are in our blood and what our blood pressure (**B**) is. Any lousy habits (**L**) in our lives, such as smoking and tobacco use, will accelerate the process of exploding plaque (**E**) accumulating in the walls of our arteries.

This second diagram reveals the dangers of a decrease in training (**T**) and an increase in roundness (**R**).

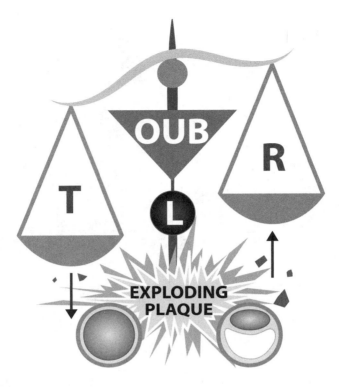

If our training decreases and our food intake remains the same or increases, we are going to have TROUBLE. This is particularly true if we consume an increased amount of saturated or trans fats starchy or refined carbohydrates. When this happens, the amount of unhealthy oil (**O**) and unacceptable sugar (**U**) in our blood increases, and our blood pressure (**B**) rises. Again, lousy habits (**L**) will accelerate this process.

In this third diagram, we see the positive outcome of increased training and the elimination of lousy habits.

There is a point as a we travel down this process where 3 of the first 5 numbers are out of range called Metabolic Syndrome (we call it meta-betes). This is your body trying to warn you that you MUST act now to reverse your path to diabetes and heart disease. One recent study revealed the cost of people with metabetes to corporations is $6528 dollars per year on healthcare, without it the average spend is under $3200 per year. So whether you look at it from a "# of conditions" or costs the result points to significant health challenges.

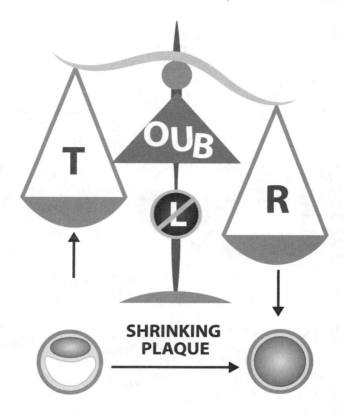

When our training (**T**) *increases*, our roundness (**R**) decreases, and the destructive oils (**O**), unacceptable sugar (**U**), and blood pressure (**B**) also decrease. This reduces the risk of plaque formation and the danger of unstable exploding plaque (**E**) in the walls of our arteries, which reduces the chances of heart disease and stroke.

Improving the quality and length of life, starts with understanding The Seven Numbers. In this book, we will carefully evaluate each of these seven TROUBLE areas and how they interact with each other to determine how well you are doing at your present point in life. We will also define your goals and help you develop a plan of action to achieve them and experience better health.

LEARN YOUR SEVEN NUMBERS

1	**T**	*Training* and fitness
2	**R**	*Roundness* or Body Mass Index (BMI)
3	**O**	*Oil* or fat levels
4	**U**	*Unacceptable Sugar* level
5	**B**	*Blood Pressure*
6	**L**	*Lousy Habits* in your life
7	**E**	*Exploding Plaque* risk within your arteries

PLAYING THE GAME OF HEALTH

Going from "I feel fine" to "I am healthy"

21

Now that you know The Seven Numbers, let's take a look at how they fit into the Game of Health. I call it the Game of Health to make things fun and easy to understand. The game we will compare achieving better health to is baseball—a favorite American pastime you are probably familiar with.

To help us understand the Game of Health, let me introduce "Mary," an example of many of the patients I see. Mary is a thirty-four-year-old mother of three young children who recently divorced and works full-time. She is on the run from 5:00 a.m. to midnight every day. She came to me complaining of headaches, fatigue and upset stomach. She is quite overweight and has type 2 diabetes. Mary is overwhelmed with work, caring for her children and the stress of life. Her diabetes is poorly managed, her blood pressure and cholesterol are dangerously high, and she smokes. Clearly, Mary's health is in serious TROUBLE.

The Game of Health was developed to help patients like Mary make the transition from being *reactive* and having her life "thrown" at her to being *proactive* and having her go after life. Somehow she needed to become aware of her health issues, understand what was causing them, and cultivate some new habits to see things change. That's the essence of the **five steps** in the Game of Health.

STEP 1
AWARENESS

STEP 2
UNDERSTANDING

STEP 3
HABITS

STEP 4
ACCOUNTABILITY

STEP 5
SHARING

5 STEPS TO SUCCESS:

STEP 1 **AWARENESS:** We discover and accept we have a problem.

STEP 2 **UNDERSTANDING:** We learn about the problem and how it works.

STEP 3 **HABITS:** We find out how the habits we have are contributing to the problem and learn new habits to overcome it.

STEP 4 **ACCOUNTABILITY:** We develop a plan of action and tell trusted friends about it, making ourselves accountable to them as we work it out.

STEP 5 **SHARING:** Finally, as we experience success, we share with others what we have and are learning, which deepens our commitment and understanding and propels us to more success.

. . . .

WE ALL START OUT IN **THE "I FEEL FINE" DUGOUT OF LIFE**

We sit back, eating, drinking and watching others play the game. It is a comfortable place. We can yell and cheer and feel like we are in the game, but the truth is we are on the sidelines. No one is looking at us. We aren't attracting attention, and the pressure to perform is minimal. In our minds, we can visualize ourselves at the plate. What stars we would be and what a difference we would make. There's only one problem: Just *thinking* about what we would, could or should do doesn't bring about the solution. It is only when we take action and get in the game that we can win.

AWARENESS IS **GETTING IN THE GAME**

The first thing that Mary and all of us need to do is make the choice to get out of the dugout and step up to the plate. As problems are "pitched" at us, we need to begin taking swings at solving them. This is where healthcare providers come in. Wisdom from doctors, nurse practitioners, physicians' assistants, dietitians, physical therapists, chiroprac-

Changes in our body are the result of a logical series of steps. By discovering these changes, we discover the quality of our health and where we are in the process. Many times when we are dealing with disease, it can be slowed or even prevented once discovered. The key is learning to look and listen to what is going on inside us. For example, the average person who develops type 2 diabetes has had "pre-diabetes," or meta-betes, for 5 to 15 years before then. During this window of time, the chance of stopping or reversing this process is possible! Where are you in the process of developing high blood pressure, lipid (fat) abnormalities, diabetes and blood vessel disease?

tors, psychologists and other licensed professionals, help us gain valuable insight and *awareness* about what is going on in our body. At this point it is vital to our success that we receive good information and encouragement. Getting in the Game takes courage!

UNDERSTANDING IS **MAKING IT TO FIRST BASE**

Once we step up to the plate and begin taking swings at our problems, eventually we are going to get a hit. Over time, as we read good books, listen to CD teachings and audio books, speak with our trusted advisors, go to visits at our doctor's office, and apply the principles to our lives, we are going to discover the right answer for the problem we are facing.

Initially, Mary was resistant to taking the time to slow down and learn about her condition. Feeling overwhelmed, she couldn't see how she could spare one more minute in her life. But she realized that she couldn't keep doing the same things and expect to get better results. Over the next several weeks, she gave up her regular TV and radio shows and listened to audio books in the car and as she did her chores at home. She also kept her office visits and began learning how cholesterol, metabetes (metabolic syndrome or pre-diabetes), diabetes, stress, and smoking affected her body. As she swung at her problems with new solutions, she began to connect and make progress.

To help you find solutions that are a hit in your life, we have made a number of resources available to you online. Go to **www.thesevennumbers.com** and print out the materials and watch the videos on the "opponents" that will try to take you out of the game. You can also download and listen to the audio teachings while you drive, exercise or relax. Don't forget to track your progress as you apply new solutions. Through *understanding* we can begin to defeat our problems and make our way to second base!

ROUNDING THE BASES RESULTS FROM DEVELOPING GOOD HABITS AND ACCOUNTABILITY

Once we have become AWARE of our TROUBLE spots and UNDER-STAND how they work in our lives, we will have successfully arrived at first base. At this point, we must ask ourselves, "What am I doing that is feeding this problem?" Discovering bad HABITS and cultivating good HABITS is one of the things that keeps us rounding the bases. By learning what the problem is and how other people have gotten into TROUBLE, we can more easily see what we need to do to change it. To help you discover these habits, use The Seven Healers Assessment at **www.mysevenhealers.com**.

The other thing that helps us round the bases is having ACCOUNT-ABILITY. While at first it may look like changing habits will be easy, we will soon discover it is not. We will need the help of trusted friends if we are going to break free from unhealthy patterns. By sharing our plan of action with others and being accountable to them to carry it out, we will experience progress. It is particularly helpful if you find someone who does what you want to start doing well. Being accountable to someone that is winning the Game of Health in that area makes it less likely that they will undermine your success.

....

Who you play the game with is really important. In **The Seven Healers** *we*

discover the powerful role others play in helping us win or lose the game.

....

So who can you lean on for support? Who will not condone your wrong choices but at the same time not condemn you when you fail? Who encourages you to be active and live healthy? What good habits can you develop to become more active and deal with stress in a healthy way? Healthy relationships and habits are major keys to winning the game of health. Once your environment supports you, instead of undermining you, you can successfully reach third base.

SHARING WHAT YOU'VE LEARNED MEANS YOU'RE HEADING FOR HOME

You now officially rock! You have figured it out and have begun to win the Game of Health. There is one step left and that is SHARING your success with others. Begin to teach a friend how you have succeeded, which will allow them to better care for his/her body.

....

We learn the most from those who are one step ahead of us and one step behind

us. Who in your life has a healthy, balanced life that you admire and can learn

from? Take some time to get to know them.

....

When I was a resident physician at Parkland Hospital, we had a saying about how to become a more competent doctor: "See one, do one, teach one." After we saw a procedure performed, we did it ourselves under the proper supervision. Once we could confidently perform the procedure on our own, we taught our co-interns and residents how they could do it. This not only allowed us to serve our fellow interns and residents, but it also forever ingrained the procedure in our minds. That's the power of sharing.

Don't look for some faraway expert to teach your loved ones. Begin to teach them yourself! As you SHARE what you have learned, your life and theirs will begin to change, grow, and succeed in ways you have never imagined.

CONGRATULATIONS!

You have successfully arrived at home plate and won the Game of Health. You became AWARE of the problem, got UNDERSTANDING on how it worked, and figured out what HABITS in your life were "feeding" it. You set new goals and recruited your friends and family to the game to be ACCOUNTABLE and help you win and keep on winning. Now you are SHARING how you won and supporting and mentoring others to become winners too. All five of these steps in the Game of Health will be used at the close of each chapter to help us better grasp and apply the principles of The Seven Numbers.

PUTTING IT
ALL TOGETHER

With an overview of The Seven Numbers under our belt and an understanding of how to play the Game of Health, let's take the next step toward better health. Along with the life-changing principles in this book, you must have a *willingness to know and understand* how your body works and a *willingness* to act upon the knowledge you learn. Knowledge without action is like having the most technologically advanced and equipped sports car but no gas to make it go. Therefore, the question is ...

ARE YOU IN **A TEACHABLE MOMENT**

I have spent my medical career watching, waiting and even trying to induce *teachable moments* in my patients. As I hear their life story, learn their habits and examine their body, I am often filled with a sense of foreboding about their future. By the end of the visit, I usually have a clear picture of what can be done to reduce the risk of major health problems in their lives. However, if my patient does not see the urgency in their situation and is not willing to take action, he is not in a teachable moment. I could try all day to convince or coerce him to do something, but it would be useless.

The fact that you are reading this book tells me that you are probably in a teachable moment. You may be are tired of not fitting into your clothes, tired of taking lots of pills, or tired of being stuck in the same set of problems. Whatever the case, you are ready to learn and are open to new choices. You are at the crossroad of life where transformation can begin, and that is exciting!

THERE ARE **NO QUICK FIXES**

Although American life revolves around fast food, fast transportation, fast computers, fast corporate changes, get-rich-quick schemes, and quick weight loss diets, there are no fast ways to fix health problems. Overcoming poor health issues is going to take time. It is a process. As Earl Nightingale says, *"Success is the progressive realization of a worthy ideal."* Quick fixes give an illusion of quantum leaps forward—something that will make up for lost time and effort. However, quick fixes act more like quicksand, keeping us stuck right where we are.

Instead of a quick fix, we are going to focus on small steps that bring transformation. In the book *TED for Diabetes* we call these steps baby steps. It may seem backwards but only by taking small steps do we make continual progress toward our goals. Change is challenging and has to come at a pace we can maintain over time. As we accomplish baby steps we gain momentum, things become more consistent and easy and we win the Game of Health! Trying to do too much too quickly leads to the "helpless and hopeless" syndrome. Slow down, identify the next small thing that needs to happen, accomplish it, and identify the next small thing. Lifestyle changes developed *little by little* bring lasting improvement. This is ageless wisdom.

THIS BOOK CAN **SAVE YOUR LIFE!**

No, there isn't any magic formula or secret code within these pages. This is simply a guidebook to lead you forward in your journey. It is designed to be interactive and enjoyable and is filled with basic principles on how the human body works and what is needed to experience good health. Also provided within these pages are real stories about real people and the wisdom of their victories and defeats. As you read, I believe your vital goals will come into focus, lighting the path to lasting and satisfying success.

There is time to take care of your health! Countless others are doing it and you can too. As you journey through each chapter, you will engage in continual fine-tuning, acquire new habits and develop a network of encouraging relationships. It only takes a few moments a day over months and years to win. Once you complete *The Seven Numbers*, I encourage you to check out *The Seven Healers*, a book that will help you understand the "inputs" in your life and how to achieve even greater success (**www.mysevenhealers.com**). But before we get into The Seven Numbers, there's one more thing I'd like to share …

A TALE OF **TWO PATIENTS**

"Bob" came to my office for a checkup after his buddy had a heart attack on the golf course. At age forty-four, Bob understood that he too might be susceptible to heart problems. He felt fine at the time and didn't think there was anything wrong, but he wanted to make sure. As we talked about his medical history, the first red flag went up when Bob told me that his father died of a heart attack in his early fifties. We then went through the results of his physical and lab tests, identifying some additional problem areas.

At the beginning of my career, I would have completed my visit with Bob by handing him a prescription for medicine and telling him to eat better and exercise. Instead, I asked him to take a TROUBLE™ Assessment home, complete it, and return in two weeks. He did and discovered a number of other areas where he was at risk. At that point, he was ready to address the problems—he was in a *teachable moment*. So we started by setting some small, achievable goals, most of which involved increasing his level of activity. I also shared some guidelines for eating called the Hand Signals of Health and started him on a vitamin and medication to lower his cholesterol. We then scheduled a follow-up appointment for six weeks later.

When Bob returned, he had experienced some improvement, which was largely due to the cholesterol-reducing medication. But his numbers showed that he was still in danger. The reason for this was that he had not figured out how to increase his physical activity in the midst of his busy schedule. One thing Bob had done in those six weeks was to take a relatively new test called a Calcium Score or Heartogram.™ Just like a mammogram reveals calcium or a mass in the breast, a Heartogram™ reveals what is going on in the heart. It shows any calcium that may have begun to accumulate in the heart arteries—a clear sign that they may be blocked.

Not surprisingly, there was some blockage, and it was more serious than we expected. The test revealed a significant buildup of plaque in one of his main heart arteries. Right away, I sent him to a heart specialist who ordered an outpatient Computer Tomography Arteriogram (CTA) Scan, which is a noninvasive coronary angiogram (it is done without sticking long needles and catheters into an artery). The test confirmed the blockage, and Bob was started on a very aggressive plan to stabilize and reverse his heart disease. This was Bob's wake-up call.

The next time I saw him, he had been able to stick with the original plan we had developed. He was also using the weekly Seven Healers™ Assessment to track his progress (**www.mysevenhealers.com**. Over the next six months, we worked together to tune-up many of his health habits. Little by little, he increased his daily activity, and as a result, he lost 30 pounds and felt much better! His cholesterol returned to normal and his blood pressure decreased. He was so inspired by the positive changes that he sent in two of his friends for a checkup. They too got on a program and began losing weight and dramatically improving the way they felt. Today, all three of them are playing golf together every Thursday, while supporting and encouraging each other to stay on track. They are playing Game of Health and winning!

Another man, whom I will call "Russell," was not so fortunate. Russell was an outstanding family doctor I had worked with when I was a resident physician. He was my mentor and the father of four very talented children. He was active in his medical group, the community, and our state professional association. He looked and felt strong and healthy. Most of his numbers were excellent. What I didn't know was that he had high cholesterol and a family history of heart disease.

In May of 1996, Russell went out for a jog and never returned. He experienced a major heart attack and was found dead on the side of the road. Hundreds of people, including his family, were stunned and devastated at his loss. A star had been taken from us without any apparent warning.

At that time, the Heartogram™ was not readily available to reveal a buildup of calcium in his heart. Consequently, there was no easy way to look and see if he had heart disease. All he had to draw from were blood tests, which don't always tell us what is going on in the heart. Speaking with his family after the tragedy, I learned that he had begun jogging again and had taken cholesterol medicine off and on. However, because he was feeling good, he often missed doses. The lack of knowledge of his true condition and lack of symptoms gave Russell a false sense of security that I have come to call the lethal "I feel fine" disease, and it proved disastrous.

Now I ask you, which scenario will you follow? Either of these people could be you—feeling fine, living life on "cruise control," possibly not realizing you are a time bomb ready to explode (this occurs a few years later in women but is the #1 cause of death. Thankfully, with a greater understanding of how these problems occur, we can find out if you are in TROUBLE and where. All you need to do is …

COMPLETE **THE TROUBLE ASSESSMENT**

Simply go to **www.thesevennumbers.com** and fill out the requested information. In order to complete the assessment, you will need your …

1. **Weight and height**
2. **LDL, HDL, and triglyceride cholesterol values**
3. **Fasting blood sugar level**
4. **Blood pressure**
5. **And an idea of how active you are, measured by a pedometer as steps per day or by the number of minutes you exercise per week.**

Once you have completed the **TROUBLE™ Assessment**, you will have a good idea of the state of your health. You'll know which areas are healthy and which areas have a problem. With this valuable information, you are ready to move into Section II and learn an in-depth overview of each of The Seven Numbers. If there are chapters that don't seem applicable to you, feel free to skim through them.

Time is of the essence. Once you know where you have issues, you are closer to averting disaster and restoring health than you think. And the best time to begin fixing the problem is now! So take a few minutes and fill out the TROUBLE™ Assessment at **www.thesevennumbers.com**.

Again, if you have any questions, concerns, or want to share your challenges or victories, I would love to hear from you. You can contact me at **www.thesevennumbers.com**. Thank you in advance for your input. Now let's take a deep breath and head into *Training*.

SECTIONTWO
THE SEVEN NUMBERS

IDENTIFYING AND ADDRESSING YOUR TROUBLE SPOTS

NUMBER ONE

"Nothing turns back the clock faster than a consistent regimen of exercise. Sure, aging is inevitable, and yes, Scripture tells us that 'it is appointed for men to die once' (Hebrews 9:27 NKJV). But those facts don't give us license to shuffle into old age, looking for a park bench to sit on. I believe we should exercise because God designed our bodies like finely tuned cars; if we never leave the garage, our batteries die. If we put our bodies through the paces, we add years to our lives—productive years that can be used in ministry or add value to the lives of others."

Jordan Rubin

Jordan Rubin, *The Great Physician's Rx for Health and Wellness* (Nashville TN: Thomas Nelson, Inc., 2005) p. 136.

TRAINING

The **T** in our TROUBLE Assessment stands for Training. It is the measure of activity we do on a regular basis and the first of The Seven Numbers that will save your life. Training includes all forms of exercise as well as physical activity. Clearly, our bodies were made to move.

Over the past several decades, the overall amount of training of Americans has decreased dramatically. With the dawn of the industrial age of the twentieth century, major changes were well underway that would result in dramatic differences in the amount of daily activity people participated in.

LIVING A **SEDENTARY LIFE**

As the industrial age brought about a greater specialization of duties, the percentage of the population involved in manual labor, particularly farming, decreased. Less manual labor meant a less active population. As a result, the amount of energy, or food, needed by these individuals also declined. Additionally, as people gained access to new luxuries, such as cars, refrigerators, electricity, and standard plumbing, the activity level declined even more and a sedentary lifestyle set in.

Think about it. With the invention of trains, planes, and automobiles, travel increased but physical activity decreased. Instead of walking or riding bikes to get somewhere, we just hop on whatever mode of transportation is available. With just about every modern-day convenience, we have accelerated the external processes around us but slowed the internal processes within us. Without regular movement, our bodies become stagnant and a breeding ground for problems.

*The **T** in our TROUBLE Assessment stands for Training. It is the measure of activity we do on a regular basis or the level of fitness you possess assessed by a fitness test. Training includes all forms of exercise as well as physical activity. Clearly, our bodies were made to move.*

THE INVENTION OF **FAST FOOD**

Along with the increased sedentary lifestyle came the advent of fast food, causing the opportunities for TROUBLE to exponentially grow. Experts believe that the average amount of food consumed by individuals living in the early days of the industrial revolution initially *declined*, but it wasn't long before this changed.

Food science quickly caught up with the changing lifestyle of Americans. With the invention of refrigeration and improvements in preservatives and packaging, foods could now be stored longer and transported farther than before. This helped the fast food industry make its way to the dinner table in the 1950s. The first of the chain restaurants to pop up was McDonalds, making its grand entrance into society in 1952. Pizza Hut followed in 1958, followed by Kentucky Fried Chicken in 1959.

This trend has accelerated to the point that we now have over 200 different fast food chains encouraging us to stop by and "have it our way." They have made high-calorie food easily available with minimal effort. Sure, it's convenient, but convenience has a price. A regular diet of calorie-dense foods like these is costly to our health and quality of life.

In addition to the proliferation of fast food is the increased amount of processed foods. Currently, food processing is so advanced that we can buy almost any food we want at any grocery store we go to. It's available in a can, in a box, or frozen. The more processed a food is, the less life-giving nutrients it contains. The transition from regularly consuming water, milk, fresh fruits and vegetables, wild game, fish, whole grain breads and rice to processed food has been dramatic.

*The industrial age has led to a **decrease** in physical activity and an **increase** in consumption. Food science has advanced to the point that high-calorie foods are readily available to us at any time. Sure, it is convenient, but this convenience is costly.*

THE INNOVATION OF **ADVANCED TECHNOLOGY**

Another major cause for a decrease in activity over the years is the development of new technology. In the 1950s, television began to find a permanent position in the American home, followed by numerous other inventions and services like VCRs, cable television, microwaves, personal computers, cell phones, the Internet, text messaging, MP3 players, and iPods. Add in a slew of video game gadgets like Atari, Nintendo Play Stations, Game Boys, and Xbox and it is easy to see how our activity level has also continued to decline.

Advanced technology has produced a "lifestyle revolution" over the past decades, and everyone has been affected to some degree. In fact, as we entered the 21st century, we super-sized our bodies to such an extent that America has become a top three contender for the most overweight and obese civilization to inhabit the earth. This is amazing, given the fact that the United Nations estimates over 40,000 people on the planet, mainly children, starve each day. This leads to one conclusion: If we are going to remain healthy, it will be by *choice*, not default. We must develop a plan to become active and stick to it.

OUR BODY NEEDS **MOVEMENT AND MAINTENANCE**

In some ways, our body is a lot like a car. In order for it to run well, we need to give it regular maintenance. We must keep the tank filled with good gas, change the oil regularly, lubricate the joints, maintain proper air pressure in the tires, and periodically check under the hood. If we drove our car 10 miles per hour for 10 to 15 years, and we gradually added 700 pounds of bricks to the trunk, which is roughly 30 percent of its overall weight, how do you think it would it run? And if we didn't do any maintenance on it until it broke down, what do you think we could expect? That's right. The car would become run-down and soon it would not work. The shocks would be shot, and the oil and fuel lines would become filled with sludge from lack of use and maintenance.

Similarly, our body needs regular maintenance and movement to remain in top working condition. Maintenance includes providing our body with good fuel in the form of good foods and good oil. Appropriate additives, such as fish oil does wonderful things for our health. They strengthen our cells and improve the wear and tear on our joints (suspension). When we exercise and get our engine up to higher speeds, we keep the fuel lines of our arteries from gumming up with exploding plaque. Regular training activates special cells in our muscles that suck up excess energy in the form of fat and sugar from the blood. Long-term training can actually decrease blockages in arteries and reverse the curse that leads to heart disease and stroke.

....

"Exercise is the best medicine for the body." —Scott Conard, M.D.

....

IT'S TIME TO TAKE **STEP IN THE RIGHT DIRECTION**

By now, you may be thinking, okay, I see the value of training. But how do I get started? The first step in the right direction is to begin to count your steps with your phone, a device like a FitBit, or very inexpensively you can get a pedometer. A pedometer is a great little device that measures how many steps a person takes in a day. They cost just a few dollars and easily clip to a person's belt or waistband. At our practice, we ask our patients to wear a pedometer from the time they get up in the morning until they go to bed. They must write down their number of steps each day so we can accurately track where they are in their level of activity.

Before we had the modern conveniences of cars, buses, or other forms of transportation, people walked everywhere, giving them an ample amount of physical activity. This is still the case for the majority of people living in third-world countries and in parts of Europe. It is estimated that the average European takes about 10,000 to 12,000 steps per day. On a recent mission trip to Africa, a group of twenty-one doctors and nurses worked at a clinic in Rwanda. Each of us averaged 15,000 to 18,000 steps a day. Unfortunately, the average American only takes about 1,600 to 3,000 steps a day. Wearing a pedometer will help you determine if you fall into this category.

It is not unusual for a caterer or courier to take over 30,000 steps a day. And an average marathon runner takes over 50,000 steps in about four and a half hours! People who are on their feet for a living are definitely high steppers.

Once you are counting your steps, it's time to start increasing your number of steps. The first goal we usually set for our patients is to move from 3,000 steps a day to 6,000. This is the break-even point. Taking 6,000 steps a day is just about 3 miles. At this point you are burning about the same number of calories you are taking in if you are eating an average diet. The next goal is to increase from 6,000 steps a day to 10,000. At 10,000 steps you are walking about 5 miles and are actually burning more calories than you are taking in. If you are intent on losing weight, this is the level you want to be at.

Many patients don't want to guess the number of steps they take in a mile, so we suggest they find a treadmill or walking track where they can accurately measure a mile. Generally, women take an average of 2,000 steps per mile and men 1,700 steps per mile. This number can be used in exchange for the number of steps to see how many calories are burned. Calories are energy units that measure the amount of energy in the food we eat. When a person walks a mile at a leisurely pace, they usually burn about 150 calories. This will be important as we go through the next several chapters and talk about the number of calories in the different foods that we eat.

Now, if you are already in pretty good shape, you may want to measure your activity by the number of minutes you exercise each week instead of the number of steps you take daily. If you are jogging, working out with weights, doing yoga or Pilates, or training for triathlons or marathons, the duration and intensity of your activity is going to equate to a different amount of calories burned. See Appendix A for the Center for Disease Control's recommended exercises and the amount of calories they expend.

At some point on your Training journey, you may want to know how you are doing in relation to others on the same path. For additional tests that you can do to assess your fitness, go to **www.thesevennumbers.com** and learn about additional ways to check your level of training.

WAYS TO INCREASE YOUR STEPS

Park farther away

Walk short distances instead of driving

Take the stairs if you are going up 1 or 2 levels

Walk the mall or a trail nearby

Do more chores like gardening and cleaning

Join a health club

Exercise with a friend weekly

THERE ARE MANY GREAT **BENEFITS OF TRAINING**

When Training goes up, Roundness comes down. And that's not the only thing that decreases. Increased Training reduces Oil (cholesterol), Unacceptable Sugar, and Blood Pressure. Although weight loss does occur, the greatest benefit patients report is an increased level of energy and a general feeling of well-being. Some people are even able to gradually get off of their antidepressants, like Prozac, Paxil, Cymbalta, Prestiq, Zoloft or Celexa. While not all patients can get off these drugs, all do see marked improvement in their overall quality of life.

In addition to feeling better is the benefit of a longer life. While at the Cooper Aerobics Center in Dallas, Texas, Dr. Steve Blair studied the effects of exercise on over 25,000 obese men and 8,000 obese women. He discovered that walking for 30 minutes a day at a moderate pace of 3-4 mph resulted in better fitness and a *longer life*. In another study, Dr. Blair looked at the longevity of four groups of people: thin and fit, thin and out-of-shape, obese and fit, and obese and out-of- shape. Who lived the longest? Yep, the fit and thin. Those who lived the shortest were the obese and out-of-shape. Surprisingly, the group that did the second best was the *obese and fit*, not the thin and out-of-shape. So, if the choice is to remain heavy and be fit or lose weight and become thin, go for heavy and fit. Research suggests that you will live longer.

How about genetics? Do they influence health more than lifestyle? Not necessarily. A study of the Pima Indians living in Arizona who became separated from their relatives in Mexico reveals that lifestyle choices can have a much greater impact on health than genetics. Mexican Pimas who worked hard over *forty* hours a week had a dramatically lower incidence of diabetes and a lower BMI than the Arizona Pimas who only worked hard about *three* hours a week. There is simply no substitute for physical activity when it comes to maintaining good health. Other benefits of regular Training include an improved quality of sleep, less lethargy and fatigue during the day, more positive outlook on life, less constipation and better digestion, decreased appetite, better food choices, and a decrease in muscle aches and pains after a period of reconditioning. All the effects of increased activity add up. Small increases result in great benefits. In short, we gain a new lease on life when we start to use our body regularly. Now you can see why we say *exercise is the best medicine for the body!*

GENES vs. LIFESTYLE

	Arizona Pimas	Mexican Pimas
Height	164	160
BMI	33.4	24.9
Hours of hard work per week	3	>40
% with Diabetes, male	54%	6.3%
% with Diabetes, female	37%	10.5%

DEVELOP **YOUR OWN EXERCISE PROGRAM**

Training is a very doable thing for any person of any age. The key is to find activities that are fun and get you moving. As you develop your own exercise program, ease into it. Don't overexert yourself or push too hard too quickly. Take your time and experiment with different things. Here are a few things to consider.

An ideal exercise program packs the greatest benefits when it includes at least three aspects: aerobics, strength training (including core building activities), and stretching. *Aerobics* are brisk, physical activities that get you breathing. They require the heart and lungs to work harder to meet the body's demand for increased oxygen and promote the circulation of oxygen through the blood.[1]

Strength training uses methods of resistance to strengthen our muscles and bones. It includes exercises using weight machines or free weights as well as push-ups and pull-ups. Strength training places pressure on the muscles, causing them to tighten and contract, drawing in energy from the blood to increase their size and power. The effects of cleaning the blood of excess sugar and fat will continue for twenty-four to forty-eight hours after a work-out, depending on its intensity. The increase in muscle that results not only provides exterior benefits to our appearance, but also helps give the support our body needs to function internally.[2]

Lastly is stretching. These exercises place particular parts of the body in a position that will lengthen, or elongate, the muscles and associated soft tissues. Upon undertaking a regular stretching program, a number of changes begin to occur within the body and specifically within the muscles themselves. Other tissues that begin to adapt to the stretching process include the fascia, tendons, ligaments, skin and scar tissue.[3]

To reap the benefits of aerobics, strength training and stretching, yoga and/or Pilates are strongly recommended as they provide all three aspects concurrently. For more ideas on Training, check out our resources online at **www.thesevennumbers.com**. As you get into the game and begin experimenting with different exercises, the program that is right for you will develop. So increase your Training and watch the TROUBLE spots in your life begin to fade.

TRAINING: PRESSING TOWARD THE GOAL

POOR	IMPROVING	ACHIEVING EXCELLENCE
Less than 45 minutes/week	45 to 150 minutes/week	Over 150 minutes/week
Less than 6,000 steps daily	6,000 to 10,000 steps daily	Over 10,000 steps daily

---

1 Medicinenet.com.

2. Livestrong.com http://www.livestrong.com/article/336536-strengthening-exercise-vs-cardio-exercise/.

3 http://www.thestretchinghandbook.com/archives/stretching.php.

PLAYING THE GAME OF HEALTH

5 STEPS TO MAKING TRAINING YOUR OWN

AWARENESS: Are you doing any Training? If so, how much do you do weekly? How about daily? Can you see how your life will improve when you incorporate more Training activities? Where are you in your fitness journey? (Go to **www.thesevennumbers.com** for a free assessment tool).

UNDERSTANDING: Do you understand how a lack of Training leads to major health problems? Which problems caught your attention most? Why? What benefits of Training would you like to experience more in your life? How are you going to start taking more responsibility for your health? What do you need to abandon to lead a healthier lifestyle?

HABITS: What habits are keeping you from participating in Training activities? Is there anything you can do while you are walking or working out that will not add more to your day but rather allow you to be more efficient? List three steps you can take to get into the Training game and become more active (i.e. get a pedometer, park your car further away from the door, or take the stairs).

ACCOUNTABILITY: Who else do you know who wants to get more active? How can you encourage and support each other? Is there a group you can join nearby, such as an exercise class, in which you can be assigned a partner and receive the benefits of mutual encouragement and support?

SHARING: Start a journal or download a free program for your computer or hand-held device. Go to **www.thesevennumbers.com** to record your journey in the game of health. Write down things you learn about health and yourself. Also, how can you be active in a way that is a model for those you care about? What about walking with your child or grandchild? The next walk may be the one they always remember and that changes their life. Remember: See one. Do one. Teach one...

NUMBER TWO

"Dieting is not the answer to keeping weight down. As you have heard many times, almost all people who diet to lose weight regain it (and more). Instead, you need to change long-term patterns of eating and physical activity. Hunger management is key. New patterns of eating must satisfy both physical hunger and the need for sensory pleasure from food."

Andrew Weil, M.D.

Andrew Weil, M.D., *Eating Well for Optimum Health* (New York, NY: Knopf, Borzoi Books 2000) p. 185.

ROUNDNESS

The **R** in our TROUBLE Assessment stands for *Roundness*. It is the measure of your weight in relation to your height—your Body Mass Index (BMI). Roundness is directly linked to Training. When our Training goes up, our Roundness goes down and with this decrease comes a decrease in our level of Oil, Unacceptable Sugar, Blood Pressure, and Exploding Plaque.

Unfortunately, just the opposite seems to be taking place in America. Roundness is on its way up. The acceleration of our portliness really hit full stride in the last ten years of the 20th century. In 1991, only four states had a population of 15 percent or more who were over 30 pounds overweight. By 1999, all but a few states had reached this mark in obesity. Indeed, we have a serious epidemic on our hands.

Sometimes it takes broadening our perspective (no pun intended) to really comprehend the condition we are in. Years ago, my wife and I took our children on a summer vacation to Paris, France. At that time, our twins were six years old and we also had a nine-year-old and a fourteen-year-old. The first thing they noticed was the apparent lack of "normal sized" people. One of our twins actually asked why all the people at the airport were "poor." He thought they couldn't afford food and that was why everyone had a thin to medium build.

We continued our study of the people, plopping down on a bench and trying to guess from which country each person had come. It actually turned out to be quite entertaining. We looked at both how they dressed and their size and then guessed their country of origin. We then examined their bags to see if they had a flag or other identifying mark. The easiest people to spot were the Americans because they were about twice the size of those from other countries. Every so often a group of Americans bounced by, and my kids would say, "American tour," and then giggle hysterically.

Our epidemic of obesity was also confirmed when I attended a recent Texas Rangers game. It was the perfect place to take pictures for my Game of Health presentation. I took over 150 photos, and most of them were of people in the 250 to 400 pound range. It saddened me to realize that there were thousands of morbidly obese individuals at that baseball game. On the way home, I asked my friends who were with me if they noticed the surprising number of obese people. Sadly, none of them had. We have become conditioned to accept obesity as normal in America.

You may wonder why I care so much if we Americans are obese. After all, what business is it of mine? To me it's not a matter of shame, guilt, or anger; it is a matter of life or death. I know the hardships these individuals will face and the pain they and their families will endure if they remain in the condition they are in for years or decades to come. That is why I care.

So what is the solution? How can we wrap our arms around the problem and begin to stem the tide of obesity in our lives? I believe the solution starts with knowing our BMI and how it affects the functioning of our body. Next, we must learn the Hand Signals of Health and begin to put them into practice at every meal. With this understanding and by establishing new habits, we can discover a healthier, longer life.

. . . .

Obesity has become an epidemic in the U.S. We have become conditioned to accept obesity as normal. An understanding of your BMI and of the Hand Signals of Health will help stem the problem of obesity.

. . . .

UNDERSTANDING **YOUR BASAL METABOLIC RATE (BMR)**

As I said at the open, *Roundness* is the measure of our weight in relation to our height. This is what is known as a person's Body Mass Index (BMI). Roundness is directly linked to Training. When our Training goes up, our Roundness goes down. Another important principle to understand is our **Basal Metabolic Rate** (BMR). This is the rate at which our body uses or *burns* energy in the forms of fat and sugar to keep us alive and functioning.

Interestingly, if you lie in bed all day and do not move a muscle, your body will still burn a fair amount of energy. The more muscle mass you have, the more energy your body burns. From our experience, we have discovered that the average man's BMR is around 2,000 calories per day, and the average woman's is around 1,400. This means a person *at complete rest* could eat this amount of calories and *not* store any extra energy in the form of fat or sugar (carbohydrates). If he or she remained inactive and began to eat more calories than his or her BMR, those extra calories would be stored in the liver as glycogen or in our fat cells as fat (adiposity). This translates to increased inches.

Maintaining a balance between calorie intake and calories burned is our goal. Unfortunately, many people are out of balance in this area, and as Billy Graham has said, "We are digging our graves with our teeth." Let's take a quick look at the digestive process and find out what happens to our food once we eat it.

. . . .

Your basal metabolic rate (BMR) is the rate at which your body burns calories in order to function. You could lie in bed all day, not moving your body, and still burn calories. The more muscle mass you have, the more energy your body burns. On average, men burn roughly 2,000 calories/day, and women burn about 1,400.

. . . .

UNDERSTANDING **THE DIGESTION PROCESS**

When we eat, the first thing we do is break down food in our mouth by chewing. When we swallow, we send ground-up food to our stomach where it is further digested by gastric acids. The digested food then moves into the small intestines where it is broken down into its smallest forms: amino acids (proteins), sugars (carbohydrates), and cholesterol and glycerols (fats). This is accomplished by enzymes released by the pancreas. These macro, or main, nutrients then pass through the wall of the small intestine and into the bloodstream.

They then go up the portal vein, which is near the pancreas, and head toward the liver and then travel to the rest of the body. As the nutrient-rich blood from the gut passes by the pancreas, hormones like insulin are released into the blood stream. They run ahead of the food to notify the organs and every cell of the body to take the nutrients out of the blood. For a more amusing illustration of this process, go to **www.thesevennumbers.com** and watch the video *Follow the Food*.

Each cell in our body is empowered to carry out its daily activities by pulling nutrients from the blood. These nutrients include oxygen, water, energy in the form of fat and/or sugar, and amino acids, which are the building blocks of all cells. They then dump the by-products, or wastes, from their work back into the blood for removal from the body. This includes things such as acids and carbon dioxide.

If the amount of energy brought into our body *exceeds* what is burned, our fat cells take up the excess and store it for future use. Our liver takes excess carbohydrates and sugar (glucose) and converts it into glycogen (2 glucose molecules) or fat (triglycerides). It then sends the fats back into the blood to be transported to the fat cells for storage. We'll go into greater detail on this in the next chapter. This protects the body from adverse effects. Fat cells store energy for the next "famine" or food shortage the body experiences. Fat is also stored in the liver, muscles, skin, tissues of the neck and upper airways, and other organs. The degree to which your body is called on to perform these functions roughly corresponds to your BMI.

ROUNDNESS AFFECTS **OUR**
ABILITY TO PROCESS ENERGY

What happened to us on our trip back from Red River is a good picture of what happens inside our body when we take in excess energy and have no room for it. When we have more fat and sugar than our body needs and all our storage places are full, our body scrambles to make room for it. In the process, our cells become overstuffed and very uncomfortable and stressed-out. This leads to a process called inflammation, which we will address more in the section on Exploding Plaque.

BMI of 19 to 24	fat cells take excess energy out of the blood and store it. They then release it during an active period
BMI of 25 to 27	fat cells are more congested and less receptive to insulin's promptings to remove excess energy from the blood
BMI of 27	the pancreas has to send out extra insulin, causing it to work overtime
BMI of 30	fat cells are resistant to taking in anymore energy. This stage quickly evolves from insulin resistance to pancreatic failure - a condition we call metabetes

At a Body Mass Index **(BMI) of 19 to 24**, our fat cells willingly take up excess energy when we eat. They then release it back into the bloodstream during an active period when our body needs it.

When we have a **BMI of 25 to 27**, things begin to change. At this point our fat cells are starting to become mildly congested and cantankerous. Depending on how much food we have ingested at a given meal, our fat cells may become less receptive to the extra energy they have to store. The more overloaded they become, the more resistant they are to the messenger hormone *insulin*, which is trying to get them to take the extra energy out of the blood.

Once our **BMI reaches 27**, the problem becomes even more pronounced. This stage is known as early metabetes. Once the pancreas sees extra energy in the form of fat and sugar coming into the body, it begins to produce additional insulin molecules to tell the fat cells to get it out of the blood and store it. Unfortunately, our fat cells are weighed down and not as responsive to insulin's promptings. As a result, the pancreas has to work overtime to make additional insulin to push the fat cells even harder to do their jobs.

Finally, at a **BMI of 30** the fat cells have had it. Even though there are numerous insulin signals floating around in the blood, the fat cells will not respond. They refuse to take in anymore energy. This stage is known as full-blown *metabetes*—the internal, stressful condition just before diabetes. It is at this point that an irreversible change occurs. Since fat cells cannot get bigger, they must *multiply*.

WHAT HAPPENS **WHEN ENERGY EXCEEDS OUR BODY'S NEEDS?**

When a person continues to force food into their system even after they are full, unruly fat cells are forced to accommodate excess energy by stretching as much as they can. When they can take it no longer, they are driven to reproduce themselves. This is similar to what we had to do on our trip home from Red River. We had too much stuff for our vehicle, so the only thing we could do was to increase our storage capacity by adding additional space on the roof. But more room does not necessarily equal a smoother trip.

At some point between the ages of eighteen months and four years old, scientists believe we have developed all of the fat cells we will need for the rest of our life. So, the only way for the body to create more space for excess energy is to create more fat cells. This is *not* a normal process, and it only occurs with a lot of tension and infighting between the fat cells and pancreas. Although additional fat cells can be shrunk down significantly after they are created, they cannot be removed even if weight loss occurs. The only method of removal is surgery.

In the meantime, as our body's tissues are bathed in high levels of insulin, they become increasingly insensitive. This condition is called *insulin resistance syndrome* (IRS). This makes the pancreas work harder and longer hours, which I will explain in more detail later. In many people the pancreas gradually burns out and metabetes turns into *diabetes*—a dangerous condition we will talk more about in the section on Unacceptable Sugar.

What else happens when the energy we take in exceeds our body's needs? At some point the body gets the bright idea to begin storing some fat in the blood vessel walls. It is possible that this too is driven by high insulin levels in the bloodstream. In any case, this key event starts the accumulation of a substance we call "plaque" in the arteries. Plaque buildup is responsible for the majority of heart attacks and strokes, which we will see as we continue our journey.

Another side effect of saturated fat cells reproducing is the additional stress of weight gain. Like the car with 700 pounds of bricks in its trunk, our body begins to ache under the added weight. Our muscles have to propel the additional mass through everyday activities. This causes additional wear and tear on our joints, leading to accelerated arthritis and/or low back pain. The tissues of the neck and throat also begin to fill up with fat, which often collapses the windpipe during sleeping and cuts off the airflow to the lungs. This common condition is known as sleep apnea.

Additional weight gain also stresses the heart. More weight means more tissue to have to pump blood to, which causes our blood pressure to rise. To compensate for this, blood vessels reinforce themselves with a fibrous matrix, becoming stiffer and more inflexible. This serves to worsen the high blood pressure problem and can ultimately lead to heart failure if not dealt with.

The bottom line is: When we continue to feed our body more energy than it needs, we inadvertently set ourselves up to fail. We pit one tissue against another, causing both to struggle to function normally. They end up compromising in order to survive. After a number of years of this internal battle, disease enters the body—or even worse, premature death. Poor health choices rob people of the joy and fulfillment that they have spent most of their lives working for. If you find yourself in this position, it's time to wake up and make some changes.

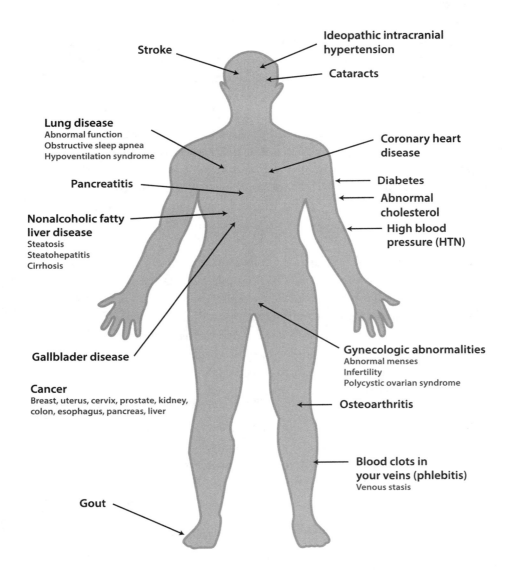

NUMBER TWO | ROUNDNESS

WHEN WE CONTINUE TO FEED OUR BODY MORE ENERGY THAN IT NEEDS . . .

Fat cells are driven to reproduce themselves

Tension and infighting between the fat cells and pancreas occurs

The body begins storing fat in the blood vessel walls, leading to plaque formation

Our heart, blood vessels, and joints are put under increased stress

THE DAY OF **MY AWAKENING**

One morning several years ago, I had my own wake-up call. While stepping out of the shower, I unexpectedly caught a glimpse of my reflection in the mirror. Just days before, I had calculated my BMI and found it to be 34.4—a number squarely in the obese category. Initially I thought, *The research scientists who developed this index table must have miscalculated their numbers. I'm not fat.* Then I hesitantly looked at a table that revealed the inevitable consequences and medical conditions that accompany obesity, and I was not a happy camper.

So there I was, standing naked and looking at my reflection in the mirror. I almost jumped out of my skin! There was a middle-aged, "jiggly," bloated man looking back at me! I said to my wife, "Wow! I have really gotten fat!" I was crushed, but in that moment I realized the BMI index must be true—I was obese. But how could this be? How had I let myself get that far out of control?

That day, I stepped out of the dugout of life and into the Game of Health. My first step was becoming keenly *aware* of my condition. I set out on my first trip around the bases, although I didn't realize that was what I was doing at the time. I had to discover what changes I needed to make. Soon I began to understand there were several reasons for my fitness demise. The biggest problem I found was that I was eating too much food. Not only did I have a *quantity* issue, I also had a *quality* issue. I desperately needed to make some changes.

THE POWER OF **CHANGING HABITS**

Losing weight is not as simple as calories in, calories out—although it is one key. What you eat, how much you eat, your activity level, the relationships in your life, the amount of sleep and water you get and your sense of purpose all play significant roles. For me, I had significant issues.

To change the condition of my body, I needed to change many of my eating habits. One of the first habits I had to eliminate from my daily routine was my 10 a.m. trip to the Cookie Bouquet. Every day I started with my first patient at 7 a.m. By 10 a.m. I was usually very hungry. The Pop Tart, candy bar, bagel, popular cereal, or white toast with jam I was eating for breakfast was not providing the nourishment I needed. These foods actually made my hunger worse because they are refined, simple carbohydrates. They flood the bloodstream with sugar and then leave a person feeling famished within a couple of hours.

That was the condition I was in around 10 a.m. Consequently, I would shoot out the back door of my office and race down to the Cookie Bouquet for a Diet Coke and a cookie. The cookie itself was probably 500 calories, which meant I would need to take about 7,000 steps to burn it off. Unfortunately, I averaged a mere 4,500 steps a day at that time—not even enough to work off the cookie. Cutting refined, high sugar calories like this out of my diet explains at least 10 of the 50 pounds that I eventually lost.

A HEALTHY SNACK

Fresh fruit is a great snack. If you can't get fresh fruit, get dried fruit. They usually come in handy, resealable packages. Dried fruit also has a long shelf life and doesn't need to be refrigerated.

In addition to *eating fewer calories*, the other key to losing weight is moving more—increasing our Training. Habits that helped me put these two principles into practice were formed one choice at a time. Finding motivation to eat healthier became easier for me once I started to pay close attention to the calorie content and portion sizes of my food. For me, this began by refocusing my attention on reading food labels.

READ THE LABEL

Cola Nutrition Facts

Serving Size: 12 fl oz

Serving Per Container

Amount Per Serving		
Calories 150	Calories from Fat 0	
		% Daily Value
Total Fat 0 g		0%
Saturated Fat 0 g		0%
Trans Fat 0 g		
Cholesterol		
Sodium 35 mg		
Potassium 46.5 mg		
Total Carbohydrate 0.15 g		
Dietary Fiber		
Sugars		
Sugar Alcohols		
Protein 0 g		
Vitamin A		
Vitamin C		
Calcium		
Iron		

Establishing a habit of reading the nutrition label on foods is a powerful step toward a healthier you. Yes, it may seem a bit intimidating at first, but with a little practice you can learn to accurately determine the amount of calories you are eating and the value they contain. For example, look at the sample food label for a common can of cola. At the top of the label you will see how the manufacturer estimates a portion. In this case, a 12-ounce can of cola is *one serving*. Often, there are two or more servings in one package. For instance, sometimes half of a candy bar is considered one portion. In a situation like that, you would need to double the nutritional information provided on the label if you ate the whole candy bar.

Food labels also reveal the total number of calories per serving. There are 150 calories in this can of cola. For an average person to burn this amount of calories, he would need to walk about 1 mile or take 2,000 steps. If you take in additional calories from snacks like this soda and do not accommodate for them by increasing your amount of training, every 23 days you will take in an additional 3,500 calories. That equals one pound of additional weight. If you did this for one year, you would gain about 15 pounds!

This simple calculation can be performed with any food. They all follow the same rules. Realize that eating calorie-rich foods increases the chance that our fat cells will become overloaded. We will learn more about calories in the sections ahead, but for now establish a habit of reading the food label. Whenever you eat, think about the caloric information and make an effort to choose better foods.

SLOW DOWN AND STRETCH YOUR STOMACH

So I began eating fewer calories, increasing my physical activity, and reading food labels. Another thing I did to improve the shape I was in was reduce the quantity of food I was eating. You too may have a problem with the quantity of food you are eating. One of the reasons we eat too much is because *we eat too fast*. By simply slowing down while we eat, we will eat less. Why? Because we will begin to feel full.

Realize that when we eat, our stomach stretches to make room for the food. This stretching stimulates a series of nerves running from the stomach to the brain, telling the brain we are full. Normally, our empty stomach is the size of our fist, so you can see that filling and stretching it is not a difficult task. Drinking a glass of water, skim milk or tea between meals is a healthy way to stretch your stomach and feel full.

....

You feel full in response to your stomach stretching. Some healthy ways to stretch your stomach and make it feel full include drinking a cup of water, tea, or skim milk or eating raw vegetables between meals.

....

Another major reason we begin to feel full is linked to the fat we eat. Fat stimulates the release of hormones from our gut, which travel through the bloodstream to the brain and tell us we are full. We will discuss fats in more detail in the next section on Oil.

Additionally, if a person has had the lap band or sleeve surgery and has a band around the top portion of their stomach, it will help curb their appetite. This means the upper part of their stomach will stretch with a much smaller meal, causing them to feel full. When we feel full, we eat less, and when we eat less, we lose weight. This is the reason for the success of this surgery many are having today. Interestingly, if we chronically overeat, the amount of stretching required to feel full will increase over time.

Armed with all this information, I began doing things to help myself resist the temptation to overeat. First, I started serving myself in the kitchen and did not bring the serving dishes with the starchy or fattening foods to the table. That way the calorie- or starch-rich food was not

Try to avoid getting second helpings. You have fed your body. Give it time to figure out that it has enough energy on board. Allow your body's hormones stimulated by your food to tell your brain you are full. If you are still hungry after 15 minutes, eat another helping of vegetables. For every helping of anything else—bread, pasta, potatoes, rice, meat—you will need to add 500 or more steps to your daily goal.

....

sitting right in front of me calling my name. If I wanted more, I would have to get up and walk to the kitchen. This gave me time to consciously pay attention to my body and decide if I really wanted a second helping. Trust me, it works. You can do it too.

LEARN TO USE **THE HAND SIGNALS OF HEALTH**

The other habit I cultivated was to use my hands to measure the serving sizes of what I was eating. Thus, the *Hand Signals of Health* were created. Food is divided into four general categories: meat, carbohydrates, vegetables and dessert. As a rule, the amount of meat we eat should be the size of the palm of our hand and as thick as a deck of cards. Vegetables—except for starchy ones like potatoes and corn—are free food. We can fill our plate with as much as we want. As for carbohydrates like bread, pasta, potatoes, corn and rice, the serving size should be no larger than the width of our fingers and about as tall as your fist.

When we finish with our first plate, we need to stop and take a time out—about 15 to 20 minutes. This allows our stretching stomach to send our brain the signal that we are full. After this allotment of time, IF we are still HUNGRY, we can then have a second portion. But seconds come with a price. Vegetables are still free, but everything else must be compensated for with additional activity or exercise. For example, a second helping of bread or meat constitutes a half mile walk per portion (750-1,000 steps).

Palm of Hand	appropriate portion of lean/low-fat MEAT. Try to make it no thicker than a deck of cards.
Width of Fingers	appropriate portion of CARBOHYDRATES, such as bread, pasta, potatoes, corn and rice. It should be about as tall as your fist.
Vegetables	except for starchy ones like potatoes and corn, these are free food. Fill your plate, but avoid high-fat sauces, butter, oils, etc.

If we decide to forgo seconds but choose to have dessert, then one *sliver* of pie or cake (no thicker than the width of one finger) equals one mile (about 2,000 steps). If we eat a *slice* (the width of two fingers), we must double that mileage, and for a *piece* of dessert (three fingers), triple it and so on.

The bottom line: Extra calories should equal extra Training or exercise. If it doesn't, extra calories will equal extra weight. When Roundness goes up, problems result. You may think this all sounds very harsh, but it is all a matter of balancing food with activity. For me, if I have had an active day and/or gone to the gym and exercised and I want a sliver, slice or piece of dessert, then I have it! Healthy living is about balance, not deprivation.

DESSERT ANYONE?

A **SLIVER**	of pie or cake, no thicker than the width of your finger = about 1 mile or 2,000 steps
A **SLICE**	of dessert, about the width of two fingers = 2 miles or 4,000 steps.
A **PIECE**	of dessert, about the width of three fingers = 3 miles or 6,000 steps

Extra calories should equal extra Training or exercise. If not, they equal extra weight.

REALIZE <u>T</u> AND <u>R</u> DIRECTLY AFFECT <u>OU</u> AND <u>B</u>

At this point you can see how a lack of Training and the gradual accumulation of a round girth set the stage for a TROUBLING future. When the amount of energy we take in continues to exceed our body's need and our fat cells are full, we create a raging metabolic war inside our body. If you fail to take heed and continue to allow your Roundness to increase and your Training to decrease, your system will begin to show signs of wear and tear. This may come in the form of high blood pressure first, followed by a cholesterol abnormality or diabetes.[4]

The third, fourth and fifth numbers that will save your life are *Oil, Unacceptable Sugar,* and *Blood Pressure.* Your daily amount of Training or activity not only affects your Roundness, it also profoundly affects these three areas. As you work through the next three sections, you will learn which numbers reveal certain things about your body.

The first step to keeping your Roundness in check is to **use a pedometer daily**. It will help you monitor and increase your quantity of Training. Remember, *all activity counts!* The break-even point is 6,000 steps, and 10,000 steps is the goal to aim for if you are trying to lose weight. If you are below these numbers, don't get upset with yourself. Make a decision to gradually increase your number of steps daily until you reach the desired goal.

I also encourage you to **weigh yourself regularly**. I do this daily, but many experts believe that weekly works better for most people. I don't lose sleep if my weight is not where I want it to be. The number on the scale is a *lagging*, not leading, indicator of good health. By checking your weight regularly, you can monitor and correct your course to ensure what you're doing is successful.

---

4 Many individuals get high cholesterol, diabetes or hypertension without being overweight or obese. For example type 1 diabetes appears to be an interaction of a person's genetic make-up with their environment, like a viral infection. We treat these conditions differently and they follow a different natural history than the path that I am writing about in this book. I would strongly encourage anyone with any of these conditions to seek medical help regarding your condition.

Another way a person can look at their weight is by looking at their waist circumference. This is particularly important because the fat in your abdomen is actually more destructive than the fat under the skin. So on average if a woman has a waist circumference of over 35 inches she has a significant amount of this abdominal fat - significantly increasing her risk of problems. Between 30 and 35 inches suggests intermediate risk. Less than 30 is usually not associated with significantly increased risk (by checking the actual OUB numbers we will see if this is the case for you). For men the numbers are > 40 inches, 36 - 40 inches and < 36 inches. These rough estimates can be a helpful guide. For instruction on how to measure your waist circumference go to **www.thesevennumbers.com**.

If you have three of these numbers TROUB out of the healthy range you have metabolic syndrome (metabetes) which means you are well on your way to diabetes and heart disease. Don't delay - get to your doctor and get your numbers to goal!

And by all means, **incorporate the Hand Signals of Health** at each meal and remember to **read those food labels**. These two activities will help you control the quantity and quality of calories you are taking into your body. Interestingly, most of us only eat ten to twenty different foods over and over again in different combinations. Take a few minutes and write a list of your main menu choices. Then over the next week, look up the nutritional information on them. Take note of how many calories they have as well as the amount of protein, sugar, fat, fiber, etc. As we learn about the remaining numbers, you will discover areas where opportunities for improvement exist. Every healthy food choice you make is a step in the right direction.

STEPS IN THE RIGHT DIRECTION

Count your steps daily.

Weigh yourself regularly.

Incorporate the Hand Signals of Health at each meal.

Read those food labels.

ROUNDNESS: PRESSING TOWARD THE GOAL

	POOR	IMPROVING	ACHIEVING EXCELLENCE
Body Mass Index (BMI)	Greater than 30	25 to 29	Less than 25
Percentage of Body Fat	Men > 25% Women > 32%	Men 19-25% Women 26-32%	Men < 19% Women < 26%
Waist Circumference	Men > 40in Women > 35in	Men 36-40 in Women 30-35 in	Men < 36 in Women < 30 in

PLAYING THE GAME OF HEALTH

5 STEPS TO MAKING ROUNDNESS YOUR OWN

AWARENESS: What is your BMI? Is it poor, improving, or achieving excellence? Do you know how many calories you are taking in on a given day? Are you taking in more than you are burning? What practical things can you do to lower your BMI and the number of calories you are taking in?

UNDERSTANDING: Can you see how a lack of Training increases Roundness and causes major health problems? Which problems caught your attention most? Are you currently experiencing any of these? What benefits of Training would you like to experience more of in your life?

HABITS: What unhealthy habits do you have that are keeping you from Training and/or causing you to over-eat? How can you eliminate these and start taking more responsibility for your health? What can you do to incorporate the Hand Signals of Health and begin reading food labels?

ACCOUNTABILITY: Who can you ask to hold you accountable regarding your Training and eating? If you have a spouse or child living with you, consider asking them for help as well, since they will most likely be with you at mealtime.

SHARING: In your Training journal, record your meals and portion sizes, as well as your activities. Do this for only one month so you can see your progress. Once you begin to see some positive progress, look for others with whom you can share what you are learning.

NUMBER THREE

"Yes, there is such a thing as *good* fat. Your body needs fat! The good types of fat heal the body and are necessary. You should eat fat every day for the health of your heart, brain, skin, hair, and every part of you. Good fat nourishes and strengthens cell membranes. Good fats include Monounsaturated fats and Omega-3 fats. ...The fats you should avoid are trans fatty acids, often called 'trans fats,' such as hydrogenated and partially hydrogenated fats. You need to limit your consumption of saturated and polyunsaturated fats."

Don Colbert, M.D.

Don Colbert, M.D., *The Seven Pillars of Health* (Lake Mary, FL: Siloam, a Strang Publication, 2007) pp. 96, 87.

OIL

The **O** in our TROUBLE Assessment stands for *Oil*. It is the quantity and quality of *fats* we have in our body. While too much of the wrong fat can be deadly, not having enough of the right fat can also pose problems. Oil plays a vital role in the human body. It surrounds every cell like an envelope, separating the inside from the outside. Oil is also the building block of our hormones—the internal messengers that tell our body how to function. Oil surrounds our nerve cells, allowing rapid communication from our head to our toes. Needless to say, trying to live life on a very low-fat (low-oil) diet is not sensible and could throw our whole system out of balance. We need healthy fat in our diet every day.

UNDERSTANDING THE **THREE MAIN TYPES OF FAT**

Saturated Fat: tends to increase the LDL (lethal) cholesterol. Hydrogenated and partially hydrogenated foods contain trans fatty acids and polyunsaturated fat that have a similar effect to saturated fat.

Polyunsaturated Fat: not as likely to cause problems, but not the healthiest form of fat.

Monounsaturated Fat: The healthiest type of fat.

Avoid saturated fat as much as possible. Limit eating polyunsaturated fat. Consume monounsaturated fat on a regular basis.

It is important to understand that fat in our food comes packaged in three main forms: Saturated fat, polyunsaturated fat and monounsaturated fat. Let's take a closer look at each.

SATURATED FAT: In general, this fat is not good because it increases the level of LDL, or lethal fat, in the body. Saturated fat becomes solid at room temperature. It is the densest source of energy we can consume. Once broken down in the body, it tends to increase the amount of LDL cholesterol in our system. LDL is the lethal cholesterol that is bad for our body. Butter, coconut oil, palm kernel oil, palm oil, and animal fat (lard) are examples of saturated fats.

POLYUNSATURATED FAT: These are the intermediate density fats that, in general, are not as likely to cause problems in the body. Polyunsaturated fats tend to be liquid at room temperature. Examples of these are corn oil, cottonseed oil, flaxseed oil, rapeseed oil, safflower oil, sesame oil, soybean oil, sunflower oil and fish oil, which also contain the beneficial nutrients DHA and EPA.

MONOUNSATURATED FAT: Of the three main fats, these are the healthiest and best choice. The most common sources are avocados, peanuts, almonds, macadamias, canola oil, and olive oil and products containing olive oil. The Mediterranean diet is high in monounsaturated fat and has attracted a lot of positive attention in the medical community over the past several years. It includes olive oil and many olive products. The Lyon Heart Study showed that patients who had a high risk of heart disease and ate the Mediterranean diet as opposed to a regular low-fat diet experienced a 70 percent reduction in the occurrence of heart attacks. The exact reason for this remains a mystery, but the healthy effects this type of diet has on blood clots and blood vessels may be partially responsible.

What about hydrogenated and partially hydrogenated oil? Good question. Hydrogenated and partially hydrogenated oil is man-made. Food engineers have discovered that by adding extra molecules of hydrogen to certain oils, it keeps them from becoming rancid. This means prepared foods last longer before spoiling, and a longer shelf life means higher profits. Unfortunately, hydrogenated fats are unstable and change into trans fatty acids once in the body. The body then handles these substances like saturated fat, making them less beneficial. It is safe to assume that if the food comes in a sealed box or bag, it is more likely to contain hydrogenated fat. These will be listed in the ingredients on any food label.

The bottom line: When it comes to fat, avoid saturated fat as much as possible and consume monounsaturated fat regularly in moderation. Polyunsaturated fats are fine with a few exceptions. If they are heated, they produce dangerous particles called free radicals that can damage our body's tissues. This occurs when foods are fried in polyunsaturated oils. So for frying foods, use olive, peanut, or canola oil.

WORST	**SATURATED FATS** **Animal fat, butter, coconut oil, palm oil**	
BETTER	**POLYUNSATURATED FATS** **Corn oil, cottonseed oil, flaxseed oil, rapeseed oil, sesame oil, soybean oil, sunflower oil**	
BEST	**MONOUNSATURATED FATS** **Olive oil, avacado oil, canola oil**	

HOW **OUR BODY BREAKS DOWN AND USES FAT**

The nutrients from food must be transported to the cells of the body. As I mentioned earlier, when food is eaten, it is broken down in the mouth, stomach and then small intestine. In the case of fats, they are broken down into *glycerol* and, to a lesser degree, *cholesterol*. These smaller droplets of fat then float up the portal vein in the bloodstream on a carrier molecule called a chilomicron. Eventually the fat, which is energy, is dropped off with cells in the body that need energy. If cells do not need energy, the fat is carried to the liver where it is repackaged and placed on another carrier, or "vehicle," called VLDL (very low density lipoproteins).

Don't be intimidated by the terms chilomicron and VLDL. They are nothing more than microscopic "trucks" that carry fat to the cells of the body that need it. Once they deliver their load to our tissues, particularly muscles and fat cells, these carriers become smaller and smaller. After a while, they become so small and so different in their composition that they are renamed remnant particles or *LDL* (low density lipoproteins). Ideally, these remnants are taken to the liver and repackaged into new VLDL.

UNDERSTANDING **HOW PLAQUE FORMS**

The formation of LDL is where the potential for problems begins. Although the most desirable destination is back to the liver, LDL can go a number of other places in the body. If there is more LDL floating around the blood than the liver can take in, which often occurs when you overeat or your fat cells are full, then the LDL molecules may pass through the wall of the blood vessel and attach itself there. This is the process known as *plaque formation* (also known as atherogenesis and atherosclerosis). Simply put, this is the buildup of fat in the blood vessel wall.

For now it is enough to say that this process will gum up our blood vessels and cause problems (check out the section on Exploding Plaque or go to **www.thesevennumbers.com** and watch the Follow the Food video). The rate at which this buildup takes place is directly proportional to the amount of extra energy (fat) left in the blood after the cells in our body absorb what they can. As I mentioned earlier, if Training decreases and food consumption remains the same or increases, the buildup of plaque in the arteries will accelerate. This is especially true if we are eating high-fat, calorie-rich foods. There is simply no place for the extra energy (fat) to go. The results are extra LDL floating around in the blood. This is a lethal situation that must be dealt with quickly, and increased Training is just what the doctor ordered.

THE AWESOME **EFFECTS OF TRAINING**

As I mentioned in the chapter on Training, one of the greatest effects of exercise is that it "cleans" our blood. When we exercise, our muscles become hungry for energy. Two sources can provide us with the needed energy. The quickest form of energy is glucose. It can be pulled out of the blood, drawn from that which is stored in the muscle itself, or extracted from the liver when it is made or from glycogen that is broken down.

Once sugar is used up, the muscle cells begin to use fat for energy. The muscles pull the fat off of the chilomicrons and VLDL carrier molecules floating in the blood and use it for energy to keep you moving. Training activates this blood-cleaning process, which continues for twenty-four to forty-eight hours *after* you exercise. The removal of excess energy from the blood helps prevent the accumulation of lethal LDL in the artery walls.

Exercise causes the body to redistribute its energy, and a key player in this process is another "carrier" molecule called HDL. This special transporter races through our body and scrapes up all the fat it can find to be used as energy. It even goes into the blood vessel walls and harvests fat! This explains why HDL is so valuable and we do everything we can to get this healthy cholesterol carrier to increase in our body. Do you know what drives up HDL levels most? You got it—exercise. Indeed, it is ***the best medicine for your body!***

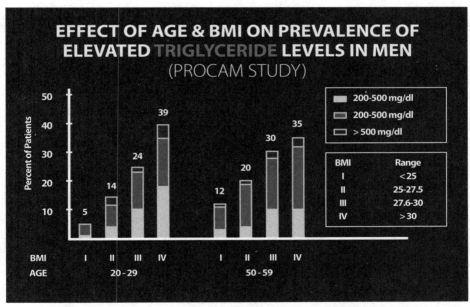

Adapted from Assmann and Schulte. In: Bjorntorp P and Brodoff B, eds. Obesity, 1992

This chart shows how fat (triglycerides) builds up in the bloodstream as we get heavier. Whether you are in your 20s or your 50s, as you become overweight and obese, the body has more difficulty "cleaning" the blood and removing the extra fats. These extra fats have a significant effect and can lead to plaque formation in our arteries.

DISCOVERING **THE ROLE OF CALORIES**

At this point, you may be thinking, *Where do calories fit into this equation? How are they connected with oil, energy and Training?* Calories are a measurement of the amount of energy in a given food. Different foods have different amounts of energy, or calories. The average man needs about 1,800 - 2,500 calories a day and the average woman needs about 1,300 - 2,000 calories a day to function properly. This can be calculated many ways. Please go to **www.thesevennumbers.com** for more information.

When the amount of activity we perform in a given day is *less* than the amount of calories we take in, we *gain* weight. When the amount of activity *exceeds* the amount of calories we take in, we *lose* weight. This is why regular Training is so vital to weight loss.

Each activity we are involved in burns a certain number of calories. For instance, the brain uses approximately 20 percent of the total number of calories we consume daily to carry out its functions. The energy it consumes is primarily in the form of glucose (sugar) because it cannot use fat as a direct energy source under normal circumstances. One would think that we could increase the consumption of sugar from our body by thinking harder or longer, but that is not the case. Evidently, the amount of energy needed to stay awake and concentrate doesn't change enough to make a significant impact on our energy consumption. Too bad!

How about walking? At a leisurely pace, this activity "burns" about 100 calories in one mile. In other words, our muscles need roughly 100 calories of energy to propel our body one mile. Said another way, our muscles will extract 100 calories of sugar or fat for every mile that we walk. Thirty minutes of dancing will burn about 140 calories, and thirty minutes of gardening will consume about 165. (For more activity values, go to **www.thesevennumbers.com**.)

So how much broccoli would we need to eat to leisurely walk a mile? The answer is about two cups because broccoli contains about 27 calories per half cup. On the other hand, a regular Snickers bar contains 240 calories. This one bar is enough to propel us 2.4 miles. How about cheesecake? One piece contains 400 to 800 calories, depending on the type. My favorite cheesecake used to be from The Cheesecake Factory until I learned it contained 880 calories! That means eating one piece of cheesecake would require walking 8 miles to burn it off. As you can see, some food packs quite a punch! We really need to count the cost before putting something in our mouths.

To increase the amount of calories we burn while walking, we can simply walk faster, further, or on more difficult terrain, such as hills or mountains. We can also burn more calories by carrying weights. This puts other muscles to work, increasing the demand for energy. Any time you use your muscles, you clear energy in the form of fat and sugar from your bloodstream. Clearly, Training produces some awesome effects and really helps trim the fat from our body.

....

Each activity we are involved in burns a certain number of calories. When the amount of activity we perform in a given day is less than the amount of calories we take in, we gain weight. When the amount of activity exceeds the amount of calories we take in, we lose weight.

....

FIND OUT **YOUR FAT NUMBERS**

Okay, so how can we find out the oil levels in our body? What do we need to do to determine how much LDL, HDL and triglycerides are floating around in our system? The answer is, go and get a *lipid panel test* done. Lipid is simply another name for fat. Your fat numbers can be determined through a simple blood test at your doctor's office, a health fair, or the blood bank where you give blood. Not only will they provide you with your LDL, HDL and triglyceride numbers, but they will also give you your total cholesterol count.

To help you understand your numbers, let's connect each one with the job it performs. I like to think of LDL as the lethal, low-down or lousy form of cholesterol. It's the potential *bad* guys, and its job is to carry fat *to* the cells for storage via the bloodstream. HDL, on the other hand, is the heavenly, happy or healthy cholesterol. It's the *good* guy that is activated by Training (exercise). Its job is to search out and scrape up fat from our body's cells and the walls of our arteries and bring it to the muscles to burn as energy. Triglycerides and free fatty acids are the names given to the particles of fat that float around in the blood to be used at any moment.

UNDERSTAND YOUR FAT NUMBERS

HDL is the heavenly, healthy, happy, good cholesterol

LDL is the lousy, lethal, low-down bad cholesterol

Triglycerides are free floating molecules of fat energy that can be directly used by our cells

When you exercise, your muscles pull energy in the form of sugar and fat from your blood

If we were to go to a highly active, agrarian (farming) society, we would find a clear connection between physical labor, healthy foods and healthy blood. Their diets would probably consist of highly complex carbohydrates, such as beans, whole grains, vegetables, and/or fruit. Their protein sources would be lean meats, like fowl, fish, wild rabbit, deer, squirrel, or free range cattle. As a result of their diet and highly active lifestyle, their HDL/LDL/triglycerides numbers would probably come back around 70/70/70. With fat numbers like these, people rarely, if ever, die of heart disease or stroke.

On the contrary, if we were to go a sedentary or low-activity society, such as the United States, we would find a clear connection between low physical activity, unhealthy foods and unhealthy blood. Here at home, our diet consists of less complex carbohydrates. Foods are more refined and processed and contain an increased amount of saturated and trans fats. Our sources of protein are fattier meats such as highly marbled beef and pork.

As a result, our HDL levels are low, and our LDL and triglycerides levels are high.

As HDL levels drop below 60 in women and below 50 in men, we know that blood vessels are less protected and more at risk to develop plaque formation. When HDL levels drop below 50 in women and below 40 in men, we know that the HDL no longer has a protective value in the body. As HDL levels drop, LDL levels rise. As LDL levels move up from 70, the likelihood that fat will get stuck in blood vessel walls increases. Keeping our HDL level high is vital. Studies like the one done on the Framingham Men reveal that even in the presence of high amounts of LDL, if HDL levels are high, the risk of death from heart attack or stroke is drastically lower.

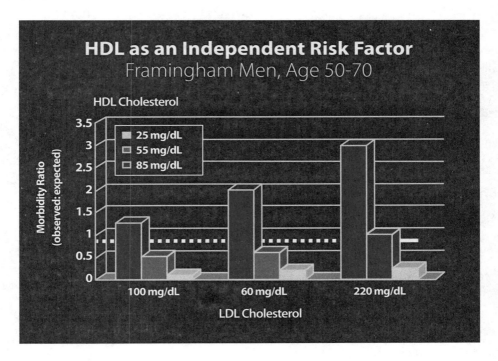

The medical industry has established two cutoff points at which they recommend medication. If a person has *never had* a heart attack or stroke, we prescribe cholesterol controlling medicine for an LDL level of 130. If a person *has had* a heart attack or stroke, we prescribe cholesterol controlling medicine for an LDL level over 100. Triglycerides are a little harder to figure out as their correlation with heart disease is not as clear. These fats are more variable and affected by many other factors, so we are less focused on them. However, if they rise over 150, they are considered too high, and treatment with a vitamin (niacin) or medication may be warranted.

The ideal fat numbers are: LDL less than 70; HDL greater than 60 in women and greater than 50 in men; and a triglycerides level of less than 90. To get the Total Cholesterol count, we take the HDL + LDL + [triglycerides / 5]. Historically, a Total Cholesterol count below 200 has been considered healthy. However, because this number alone can sometimes be misleading, we use a ratio of the Total Cholesterol / HDL to get an accurate reading of our fat levels. This lets us know how many good guys (HDL) we have in relation to the bad guys (LDL). The Ideal ratio we aim for is less than 3.5. Any ratio greater than 5 is a major concern that may require intervention.

....

The ideal fat numbers are: LDL less than 70; HDL greater than 60 in women and greater than 50 in men; and a triglyceride level of less than 90.

....

MAKE SURE YOU **READ THOSE LABELS**

Next to increasing your Training, watching what you eat is a major key to maintaining healthy oil levels. I've said it before and I'll say it again: Make sure you *read the labels*. I know they may seem a bit intimidating at first, but they are really not hard to understand. Take a look at the food label for a pre-prepared steak and biscuit meal. For now, let's focus our attention on the fat and calorie content.

Steak with biscuit
Nutrition Facts

Serving Size: 1 serving

Serving Per Container

Amount Per Serving		
Calories 455	Calories from Fat 234	
		% Daily Value
Total Fat 26 g		0%
Saturated Fat 6.9 g		0%
Monosaturated fat 11.1 g		
Polynsaturated Fat 6.4 g		
Cholesterol 25 mg		
Sodium 795 mg		
Total Carbohydrate 44.4 g		
Dietary Fiber 0 g		
Sugars 0 g		
Protein 13.1 g		

As you look at the label, notice the total calories— 455. This is nearly one-third of the total daily recommended number of calories for a woman. Under the fat section, we see the three types of fat broken down. In this instance, the *saturated fat* is 6.9 grams, the *polyunsaturated* fat is 6.4 grams, and the *monounsaturated* fat is 11.1 grams. As a general rule, you want to keep the saturated fat as close to zero as possible (< 7 percent for daily calories is the American Heart Association guideline). If it is a fried food or contains hydrogenated or partially hydrogenated oil, you want to keep the polyunsaturated as close to zero as well. I do want to give you a major warning: Fat in any form has the most calories per gram. There are 9 calories per gram of fat as compared to 4 to 5 calories per gram of carbo-hydrates and proteins.

This means for one gram of fat, you have to walk twice as many steps as you would to burn one gram of protein or carbohydrates. This is the reason why the popular diets during the 1980s and 1990s attempted to lower the calories by lowering the fat. The only problem with this is that fat provides the body with one of the strongest cues that it is full. This explains why someone on a low-fat diet will often experience a lot of hunger throughout the day. I have experienced this myself.

To get around this, I often eat a fat-containing snack around 4 p.m. Included in the snack is a handful of almonds—a good source of healthy monounsaturated fat. I found that eating the snack without almonds left me unbearably hungry in a short amount of time. Adding almonds helped me feel full longer. This allowed me to come home at night with my appetite under control instead of like a ravenous bear prone to overeating.

HEALTHY SNACK ITEMS

Almonds, pumpkin seeds, macadamia nuts, soy nuts

Plain yogurt (I like Greek yogurt.)

Applesauce with cinnamon, bananas with cinnamon and agave nectar

Apples, pears, grapes, strawberries, blueberries

As a general rule, you want to get 20 to 30 percent of your total calories each day from fat. If you are on a 1,500-calorie diet, this is about 300 to 450 calories or 33 to 50 total grams of fat each day. Eating a 26-gram steak and biscuit meal will wipe out most of the day's allotment. Remember, it is easier to avoid TROUBLE than to fix it after the fact. So read those labels. They will help you *buy* better foods and therefore *eat* better foods.

So there you have it. That is an overview of Oil in a nutshell. I encourage you to read over this chapter a couple of times to familiarize yourself with the information, and form a new habit of reading food labels. With the right understanding you can figure out what will satisfy your body to increase your good fat consumptions and steer clear of the bad ones.

OIL: PRESSING TOWARD THE GOAL

TYPE OF FAT	POOR	IMPROVING	ACHIEVING EXCELLENCE
LDL [Lethal, Bad]	Greater than 130	70 to 130	Less than 70
HDL [Heavenly, Good]	Women: Less than 50 | Men: Less than 40	Women: 50 to 60 | Men: 40 to 50	Women: Greater than 60 | Men: Greater than 50
Triglycerides	Greater than 150	90 to 150	Less than 90
HDL/Total Cholesterol Ratio	Greater than 5	3.5 to 5	Less than 3.5

PLAYING THE GAME OF HEALTH

5 STEPS TO ENSURE YOU ARE GETTING THE RIGHT QUANTITY AND QUALITY OF OIL

AWARENESS: Are you eating foods with unhealthy, saturated fats? Are you eating any foods with good, monounsaturated fats? Look in your cupboard and take note of the different types of cooking oils you have. What is your HDL (good fat) level and your LDL (bad fat) level? If you don't know, a trip to your doctor for some blood work is definitely in order.

UNDERSTANDING: Do you have a clear picture of the problems associated with consuming saturated fats? Can you see how eliminating saturated fat and increasing your consumption of healthy, monounsaturated fat can improve your quality of life? What are some ways that you can eliminate some of the more dangerous oils in your diet?

HABITS: One of the best habits to develop is planning a weekly menu. Go to a local bookstore or supermarket and look through some "cooking light" cookbooks. Get ideas of better, healthier ways to prepare your meals. Plan breakfast, lunch and dinner for the week, using healthy, monounsaturated fats whenever possible. Make a quick list of fast food restaurants that offer the healthiest foods.

ACCOUNTABILITY: Get together with some of your friends and put together a list of recipes that use less unhealthy oil and more healthy oil. Start experimenting together. This builds healthy social bonds, releases good hormones (oxytocin) and will improveyour health!

SHARING: Once you become more aware of the importance of good oils and understand the dangers associated with unhealthy fats, begin to share with friends and family some of the insights you have learned. If you are bringing a dish to a family reunion or a get-together with friends, bring a healthier alternative, such as a veggie or fruit tray instead of a casserole or dessert.

Don't Die-it —Live It!

Without a good understanding of fats and why we need them, many Americans have fallen prey to myriads of quick-fix, fad diets that have not worked. Consequently, they have been left feeling frustrated, hopeless and sometimes ill. To help you avoid this as well as other harmful effects, here are a few things to consider about fad diets and eating habits.

Most diets oversimplify complex issues. Not all of us are heavy for the same reason. Some of us are overweight because we overeat relatively healthy food. Others eat too much fat. Some are on a sugar roller coaster or take medication that leads to weight gain. Others simply don't exercise, or feed their anxiety, stress, or depression with food. For many, it is a combination of two or more of these reasons. True change comes when we look at an overview of our behavior and make adjustments in several areas.

Most diets teach a gimmick. Oh, it may work, but it does not lead to a lifestyle change in the way you eat and exercise. Sure, we can eat only grapefruit for a week and lose 7 pounds. But more than likely, we will quickly end up in the same old eating pattern as before.

Most diets are impossible to maintain. They place restrictions on your eating that are impossible to continue for a long period of time. I mean, who can eat only sausage and eggs or oatmeal with skim milk for the rest of their lives? Eliminating carbohydrates, protein or fat will never work. We all need a variety of options to be successful.

Most diets add activities to already overcrowded schedules. This includes things like joining a gym, preparing special meals, exercising for extended periods or going to group meetings. We all live full, and sometimes hectic, lives. Just adding more activities is not the answer. We must take an honest look at what we're doing and make some adjustments to be successful.

Most diets eliminate fast food. Knowing the highly active American lifestyle, this will more than likely not work. Knowing what we are going to order *before* we pull up to the drive-thru window, reducing the number of times we eat out or learning to substitute better choices is more realistic and doable.

Most diets use a "one-size-fits-all" plan. But because each of us is a unique person, each body has its own set of rules. Add to this the changes in how our bodies operate through the different seasons of aging, and it is easy to see how one set diet regimen is not going to work for everyone. A post-menopausal woman is not going to respond to a diet the same way a twenty-five-year-old man will. Experimenting with different things until we find what works is the answer.

Most diets are built on unrealistic quick fixes. As I said earlier, there are no shortcuts to good health. It is through making a series of good choices over an extended period of time that results will come. Programs built on long-term, gradual, lifestyle changes will take weight off and keep it off.

For any diet to be successful, the suggested changes must be grounded in truth. If it sounds too good to be true, it probably is. Another major key to success is securing the support of your family and friends. Social support is vital; without it, no one will succeed. For more thoughts on this subject go to **www.mysevenhealers.com**.

NUMBER FOUR

"…Has anyone stopped to think about what happens to excess sugar that is the end product of carbohydrate metabolism? Some sugar is used in our blood to maintain an adequate circulating blood glucose level, and some will replenish glycogen stores in the liver and muscles. But what happens to the rest? It is converted to fat. Yes, most of our body fat comes from ingested sugar, not ingested fat. This conversion is facilitated by the hormone insulin."

H. Leighton Steward, Morrison C. Bethea, M.D., Samuel S. Andrews, M.D. and Luis A. Balart, M.D.

H. Leighton Steward, Morrison C. Bethea, M.D., Samuel S. Andrews, M.D. and Luis A. Balart, M.D., Sugar Busters! (New York, NY: The Ballantine Publishing Group, 1998) p. 102.

UNACCEPTABLE SUGAR

The **U** in our TROUBLE Assessment stands for *Unacceptable Sugar*. The numbers connected with Unacceptable Sugar show you how well your body is dealing with your intake of carbohydrates. Our body definitely needs sugar for energy to function properly. But too much sugar is a recipe for disaster we want to avoid.

One of the most interesting and controversial issues in medicine today is the effect refined carbohydrates, such as table sugar, has on our bodies. In his book *Sugar Blues*, William Duffy got this controversy going with his proclamation that the introduction of sugar has led to the collapse of every great society from Egypt to the present day. While many medical experts viewed this as fringe sensationalism, the publication of the book *Sugar Busters!* by H. Leighton Steward, Morrison Bethea, MD, Samuel Andrews, MD, and Luis Balart, MD, rekindled the flame.

Whether Duffy's claim is totally on target or not, the dramatic increase of refined sugar consumption and starchy foods by Americans is very concerning. According to the U.S. Department of Agriculture, the average American ate 5 pounds of sugar per year in 1900. In the year 2000, the estimated average sugar consumption per person was 163 pounds. That's a 3,260 percent increase in 100 years! Our sweet tooth is definitely out of control.

....

The numbers connected with Unacceptable Sugar show you how well your body is dealing with your intake of carbohydrates.

....

WHERE IS ALL THAT **SUGAR COMING FROM?**

How on earth could a person get all that sugar in their diet? Most of us may use a teaspoon here and there but never 163 pounds! Unfortunately, we are getting more sugar from our diet than we realize. As we have already discovered, processed foods are high in salt and sugar. If it is boxed up, wrapped in cellophane, and stored on a shelf for months at a time, it is highly processed and more than likely full of sugar, salt or fat. Sugar is often hidden under different names, such as corn syrup, high fructose corn syrup, maltose, dextrose, sucralose, and maltodextrin. If you read the labels, you will find it. These are nothing more than refined, and in some cases chemically engineered, sugars.

Prepared food items made from flour and sugar are another major source of sugar in our diet. This includes things like cookies, cakes, pies, candy, chips, ice cream, and soft drinks. Starchy foods are the other culprit. These come in the form of bread, pasta, corn, rice, and the biggest source, potatoes. In the past few years, there has been an increased emphasis on potatoes in our diet.

When we eat starchy foods like potatoes, pasta and corn, our body breaks them down into individual glucose molecules. These molecules quickly flow into the blood and raise our blood sugar level dramatically. Although this simple sugar is the main type our body uses for energy, too much sugar too fast puts a tremendous amount of stress on our body.

· ·

The average American ate 5 pounds of sugar in 1900. Today we eat about 163 pounds! In addition to refined sugars found in cookies, cakes, pies, candy, chips, ice cream, and soft drinks, the majority of our "sugars" come from bread, pasta, corn, rice and potatoes.

· ·

CARBS BREAK DOWN INTO **THREE MAIN FORMS OF SUGAR**

So, you might be thinking, *If sugar is a carbohydrate and carbohydrates have only half the calories of fat, why is eating carbs and sugar a problem?* The answer is not as simple as you might think. When we eat carbohydrates, they are broken down into three main forms of sugar: *glucose*, the most common; *fructose*, from table sugar, fruit and fruit juices; and *galactose*, from milk. Some carbohydrates, like fiber, cannot be broken down by our stomachs. Consequently, they form a significant portion of the bulk in our bowel movements. We will talk more about this later.

Once these sugars are absorbed into the bloodstream, they pass by the pancreas, which notifies the cells of the body via a hormone called *insulin* that they need to absorb the sugar from the blood. The amount of insulin produced and released depends upon two things: the amount of sugar ingested and, more importantly, how rapidly it is absorbed into the bloodstream from the gut. The rate at which our blood sugar rises and the effect a food has on insulin production is known as the *glycemic index* of food.

If we eat a high sugar snack all by itself—like a cola and a candy bar—then our blood sugar level rises very quickly. If we eat the same cola and candy bar with some broccoli and Metamucil, then our blood sugar will rise more slowly because the fiber slows the absorption. Likewise, if we eat the same sugary snack with two tablespoons of lard (or a donut), the fat will also delay the absorption. So the effect of a given amount of sugar on your body varies according to what you eat with it. Both fiber and fat slow the absorption of sugar. Protein also has this effect. This is an important principle that, when applied, will help you achieve a balanced diet.

CARBOHYDRATES ARE BROKEN DOWN IN THE BODY INTO THREE MAIN SUGARS:

glucose: *the most common is derived from table sugar, potatoes, corn, rice, pasta and flour.*

fructose: *from table sugar, fruit and fruit juices.*

galactose: *from milk*

UNDERSTANDING **THE IMPORTANT ROLE OF INSULIN**

Insulin's primary job is to pull energy out of the blood. It prevents accumulation that leads to things like dehydration or much worse, falling into a coma. It does this by signaling the cells in our body to take the glucose out of our bloodstream and into the cells. It also tells the liver to quit making glucose. Its goal is to maintain the balance of energy within the blood in a narrowly defined range. You may not realize it but your liver makes up to half of the glucose your body needs every day. This helps explain why you may go to bed with a lower blood sugar level than the one you wake up with in the morning.

Our body begins to experience problems when our fat cells and other cells become resistant to taking in energy from the bloodstream. This is called *insulin resistance syndrome* (IRS). As we discussed earlier, this begins at a BMI of around 25 - 27 and intensifies with weight gain. At this pivotal point, an internal conflict between the bloodstream and the cells begins. They argue over what to do with the excess energy. In response to the failure of the glucose levels to drop, the pancreas makes more insulin, which pushes the cells harder, which leads to increased stress (and inflammation), which drives the development of diabetes, heart attacks, and strokes.

Once this situation has gone on for years, the pancreas begins to fail. This leads to a second problem: low blood sugars, or hypoglycemia, three to four hours after eating. In a normal pancreas, a bolus of insulin is released right after eating to bring down the blood sugar. When the pancreas begins to fail, it releases *less* insulin initially, but then it has to produce more insulin over the next 2 hours or so. In this situation, the extra insulin causes the person's blood sugar level to drop too low three to four hours after eating. Symptoms of hypoglycemia include feeling dizzy, weak, nauseated, shaky, and even confused. The brain detects this change because it is dependent on glucose for energy. Immediately, the brain sends out a message that it needs food. This prompts the person to eat another snack, which is often high in carbohydrates. This keeps the roller coaster ride of sugar highs and lows going.

....

Insulin's primary job is to signal your cells to take energy out of the blood. The amount of insulin your body produces depends upon the amount of sugar you ingest. Elevated insulin levels are connected with increased rates of diabetes, heart attacks, and strokes.

....

Millions of Americans ride this ride every day. I did myself many years ago, and I can tell you that it is not very amusing. I used to start my day by eating a high-carbohydrate breakfast that usually consisted of a bowl of cereal and a piece of white toast, a roll or a muffin. By eating a high-carbohydrate, low-protein breakfast, I set myself up for the need to snack throughout the day. I still remember my 10 a.m. "cookie runs" and my afternoon candy bar and cola breaks. As I mentioned earlier, this was a major problem for me and it accounted for a lot of my weight gain.

A group of doctors in Boston did a study a few years ago on the effects of eating a high-carb-only breakfast. They fed a select group of children a high-carbohydrate breakfast, which means it had a high glycemic index and was quickly absorbed into the bloodstream. For the next twenty-four hours, the doctors monitored how much the children ate. They then changed the children's diet by substituting protein for a portion of the high-carbohydrate breakfast. This lowered the glycemic index, thereby decreasing the rate at which the sugar was absorbed into the bloodstream. The effect was obvious. The children ate less and took in fewer calories the following day.

The moral of the story and the rule of thumb we should all follow is clear: A balanced diet that includes carbohydrates, protein and healthy fat will produce a more satisfied appetite. This will lead to less food consumption and give our pancreas some rest. The daily recommended balanced diet includes 40 to 55 percent high-quality carbohydrates, 20 to 30 percent fat and about 20 percent protein. Oh, and don't forget 25 to 30 grams of fiber. Your body will thank you for it!

....

If you take in fewer carbohydrate- and sugar-laden snacks, you will often consume fewer calories in a day. A balanced diet of 40 to 55 percent high-quality carbohydrates, 20 to 30 percent healthy fat and about 20 percent protein will lead to a more satisfied appetite and less food consumption.

....

EATING CANDY IS **NOT SUCH A SWEET IDEA**

Let's take what we've learned so far and apply it to a typical vending machine snack. Look at the label from a bag of M&M's. As you can see, it contains 236 calories, which will take roughly 4,720 steps for the average woman to walk off. The label also shows that it has 10 grams of fat, and while some of it is the less dangerous monounsaturated fat, it also has a lot of saturated fat, which is worrisome.

Under carbohydrates, we see three things. First, it lists the amount of dietary fiber. Amazingly, M&M's have fiber—albeit only 1.2 grams. The average American eats about 12 to 18 grams of fiber per day according to the United States National Academy of Sciences, Institute of Medicine. The daily recommendation is 25 to 30 grams. We would have to eat a lot of M&M's to take in that amount of fiber! Better sources of fiber include fresh fruit and vegetables, whole-grain bread, brown rice, soybeans, and legumes like beans and lentils.

M&M's Nutrition Facts

Serving Size: 1.69 oz pkg (69 pcs)	
Serving Per Container 1	
Amount Per Serving	
Calories 236	Calories from Fat 91
	% Daily Value
Total Fat 10.1 g	0%
Saturated Fat 6.3 g	0%
Monosaturated fat 3.3 g	
Polynsaturated Fat 0.3 g	
Cholesterol 7 mg	
Sodium 29 mg	
Total Carbohydrate 34.2 g	
Dietary Fiber 1.2 g	
Sugars 26 g	
Protein 2.1 g	

Next, notice that the sugar content is 26 grams. This is about 8½ teaspoons—an amount that will definitely do a number on your pancreas and on your blood sugar level if you are a person with diabetes. As a general rule, I try to avoid foods that have more than 10 grams of sugar per serving. Although impossible to do at times, it's a worthy goal.

Finally, notice that the *total carbohydrates* is 34.2 grams. This is 9 grams more than the sum of fiber and sugar. Usually a difference like this is attributed to some form of starch. In this case, however, the hidden source of sugar is corn syrup, a particularly troubling form of carbohydrate that not only raises the blood sugar level but also the triglyceride level. It increases the likelihood of the LDL in your blood forming plaque. Again, this is the really dangerous situation we've talked about that leads to strokes and heart attacks.

....

The average American eats about 12 to 18 grams of fiber per day. The daily recommendation is 25 to 30 grams. Fiber not only slows the release of sugar into the bloodstream, it also cleans the cracks and crevices of the large and small intestines, removing toxic bacteria that cause disease.

....

That being said, it is important to calculate the non-fiber carbohydrates in the foods we eat. To do this, simply take the total carbohydrates and subtract the amount of fiber. The higher the amount of non-fiber carbs, the less likely we should eat it. Once we start watching and learning the numbers, it becomes evident that the best carbohydrates are those that are more complex. These include foods like fresh fruits and vegetables, brown rice, sweet potatoes, and whole-grain breads and pastas. An average banana and apple each have about 5 grams of fiber, and good 100 percent whole-grain bread has about 2 to 4 grams of fiber per slice.

Keep in mind, the total amount of calories we want to get from carbo-hydrates is 40 to 55 percent. On a 1,500-calorie diet, that is 600 to 825 calories from carbohydrates, which equals 150 to 206.25 grams per day. Since there are 4 calories in each gram of carbohydrate, we divide the 600 to 825 calories by 4 to get the total number of grams of carbohydrates to aim for daily.

To put all this in perspective, a bag of M&M's has 34.2 grams of carbo-hydrates, and a twenty-ounce cola has 60 grams. Combined as a mid-morning snack, these two items together pack 94 grams of carbs, which is about half of our daily total. One bag of M&M's and a cola would require 9,720 steps to undo! That is definitely something to chew on. Remember, it is always better to prevent a problem than to try and undo one after you have it.

The total number of calories from carbohydrates we should consume in a day is 40 to 55 percent. This means if we are eating a 2,000-calorie diet, we should take in no more than 800 to 1,100 calories of carbs. This equals about 200 to 275 grams. Total Carbs = Fiber + Non-fiber Carbohydrates.

WAYS IN WHICH **YOUR BLOOD IS TESTED AND DIAGNOSED**

Figuring out how our body is handling sugar can be a little tricky. It does an amazing, meticulous job of keeping things under control. Therefore, in order to accurately determine its ability to process sugar, our blood sugar level must be checked both before meals and two hours after the initiation of a meal. This is called the pre-prandial reading and the post-prandial reading, and it is done with a glucometer.

If you check your blood sugar before a meal, it will be normal (<100), unless you are already a a person with diabetes. The first sign that your body is having difficulty controlling sugar levels will be an increase in the amount of insulin in your bloodstream. Your insulin level can be measured directly (before eating) or as a blood test called the c-peptide (also before eating), which we will talk more about in just a bit.

If your body continues to lose the ability to process sugar and your pancreas becomes fatigued, the next change will be a rise in the *after-meal* blood sugar level to above 140 mg/dl at two hours. Next, if stress from Unacceptable Sugar and excessive fat in your system continues, your *before-meal* (fasting) blood sugar level will begin to rise above normal, but this will be months to years after the *after-meal* rise occurs.

THE GLUCOSE TOLERANCE TEST

To test your body's ability to handle sugar, your doctor will probably have you drink a bottle of glucose water that contains 75 grams of glucose. He will then check your blood sugar two hours later. This is called the *glucose tolerance test*. It gives you an idea of how well your pancreas can deal with a sugar load. If it is producing the right amount of insulin, you will have a normal blood sugar level after two hours. You could actually do this test at home. Simply drink a 20-ounce cola, wait a couple of hours, and then check your blood sugar level using a glucometer, or glucose monitor. You can borrow one from a friend who has diabetes or purchase one at almost all pharmacies. It's not a perfect test, but it will give you an idea of how your pancreas is working.[5]

The results from a glucose tolerance test will be one of the following diagnoses:

Normal Fasting Glucose and Response

A person is said to have a normal glucose when the fasting glucose is <100. A normal response is when the 2-hour glucose level is less than or equal to **140 mg/dL**.

Impaired Fasting Glucose

When a person has a fasting (before meal) glucose equal to or *greater than* 100 mg/dL and less than 126 mg/dL, they are said to have *impaired fasting glucose*. This is considered a risk factor for developing diabetes in the future. A person with this diagnosis is not labeled as having diabetes, but they will probably be tested again in the near future.

Impaired Glucose Tolerance

A person is said to have *impaired glucose tolerance* when the 2-hour glucose results from the oral glucose tolerance test are *greater than or equal to* 140 mg/dL but less than 200 mg/dL. This is also considered a risk factor for developing diabetes in the future.

---

5 http://www.endocrineweb.com/conditions/diabetes/diagnosing-diabetes

Diabetes

A person has diabetes when the fasting glucose is above 125 or the oral glucose tolerance test shows the blood glucose level after 2 hours is *equal to or more than* **200 mg/dL**. These results must be confirmed by a second test on another day.

Both *Impaired Fasting Glucose* and *Impaired Glucose Tolerance* diagnoses are associated with low HDL (good) cholesterol, high triglycerides, high blood pressure and obesity—especially abdominal or visceral obesity. Moreover, regarding both the *Impaired Glucose Tolerance* and *Diabetes* diagnoses, there has recently been discussion about lowering the upper value to 180 mg/dL. This would enable more people to be diagnosed with mild diabetes and allow earlier intervention and hopefully prevention of diabetic complications.

BLOOD SUGAR DIAGNOSIS	AMOUNT OF SUGAR (GLUCOSE) IN BLOOD	HgbA1c OR 3 MONTH AVERAGE SUGAR
Normal Fasting Glucose	Less than or equal to 100 mg/dL	Less than 5.8
Impaired Fasting Glucose	Greater than 100 mg/dL and less than 126 mg/dL	5.8 to 6.4 grams/dl
Impaired Glucose Tolerance	Greater than or equal to 140 mg/dL but less than 200 mg/dL	5.8 to 6.4 grams/dl
Diabetes	Equal to or more than 200 mg/dL on two separate occasions	6.5 or greater

THE C-PEPTIDE OR SERUM INSULIN

As I mentioned, the first sign that your body is having difficulty controlling sugar levels will be an increase in your insulin or c-peptide level. The blood test conducted to follow the rate of insulin production in your body is called a *serum insulin* or *c-peptide level*. After an 8 to 12 hour fast, before eating any food, the amount of insulin in the blood is measured. This gives a good idea of how hard your pancreas has to work to keep your blood sugar controlled. The exact values for this test are a little sketchy, but most clinicians use a blood insulin level of less than 10 as normal. This is equivalent to a c-peptide level of 1.8. If the blood insulin level is greater than 20, there is a significant stress being placed on the system. This is a c-peptide level of over 3.

Let me try to put this in perspective. Let's say a normal c-peptide reading of 1.8 and a blood insulin level of 5 is equivalent to an 8-hour workday for an adult. How long do you think you would last if you were working 16 hours a day straight? A c-peptide level of 3.6 and blood insulin level of 10 to 14 are equivalent to a 16-hour workday. How long do you think you would last if you had to work 24 hours a day? That is what a c-peptide reading of 5.4 and blood insulin level of 15 are equivalent to.

The amazing thing is, our pancreas will often keep going for 5, 10, or even 15 years before it burns out and a person develops diabetes. Strangely, there are some people whose pancreas works this hard and it *never* burns out— they never get diabetes. Unfortunately, what these individuals do acquire is heart disease and strokes. Hopefully you are getting the picture. Unacceptable Sugar levels lead to an internally (metabolically) stressed body and debilitating disease—a place you don't want to go.

THE THREE MONTH BLOOD SUGAR (GLUCOSE) TEST

The HbgA1c blood test is a simple test that measures the average blood sugar in your blood stream for the past three months. If it is under 5.8 you have been under good control. From 5.8 to 6.4 your blood sugar has been higher than normal, and if it is above 6.5 you are a person with diabetes. How does this work? Imagine it this way. Suppose we are manufacturing cars in a factory. As the cars are produced they are carefully closed. If there were variable amounts of smoke in the air at the factory during their production, then we could take cars that were produced at the factory for the last three months and reopen them. As we did if we averaged the smoke in them we would know, on average how much smoke was in the factory. Now picture the cars as red blood cells and the smoke as sugar in the blood (the "air" in the bone marrow). If we check the sugar in the red blood cells produced over the past three months this tells us the average blood sugar in the body.

WHEN ALL ELSE FAILS, **LOOK IN THE MIRROR**

One of the quickest ways I have found to determine what is going on inside your body is to take a good look at yourself in the mirror. Now, I'm not talking about looking at your face. I'm talking about looking at yourself in a full-length mirror without any clothes on before or after your shower. Just stand naked sideways and look at yourself. What do you see? Where are you storing your fat?

In the *presence* of high insulin levels, our body tends to store fat in our stomach, creating the so-called "beer belly." It also gives us an **apple**-shaped appearance. The bigger your belly bulges, the more likely you have a similar bulge of plaque inside your arteries. This is the immediate predecessor of a heart attack or stroke. If your fat is in your belly, watch out. It is more than likely a sign that you are overindulging in sugar. This includes foods such as bread, rice, pasta, potatoes, corn, cookies, cakes, candies, chips, pies, soft drinks, or beer, which contains maltose—another form of sugar.

In the *absence* of high insulin, especially in women, excess fat migrates more to the hips and buttocks, creating a **pear**-shaped appearance. If you

---

6 http://predictmyrisk.com/

are storing fat in your buttocks and thighs, your insulin level is not as high. However, you are still at risk of experiencing fatigue and joint destruction. If you have both an apple and pear shape, you are storing fat in both areas. You have a significant challenge in front of you, but you can see your situation change once you put your heart and mind to it.

If you look in the mirror and see a large gut, take a look at your diet. You will probably find a lot of processed food like bread, pasta, potatoes, corn, rice, cookies, cakes, candies, chips, beers or colas. Realize that if this is the case, your pancreas is working overtime to produce insulin and remove excess sugar from your bloodstream. Make up your mind to change your menu choices to healthier foods and increase your amount of *Training*. If you don't, the day your pancreas cannot keep up with the pressure of your diet will be the day you become a person with diabetes. So don't wait! Get out there and shrink that gut!

APPEARANCE IN MIRROR	YOU'RE STORING FAT IN	THIS INDICATES
Apple-shaped	**Stomach/Belly**	**High insulin / c-peptide levels**
Pear-shaped	**Hips & Buttocks**	**Low insulin / c-peptide levels but too many calories**
Apple- and Pear-shaped	**Belly, Hips & Buttocks**	**High insulin / c-peptide levels and too many calories**

IT IS **NEVER TOO LATE**

In 2001, a group of Finnish doctors underwent a landmark study, publishing their findings in the New England Journal of Medicine. They took two groups of people who were at high risk for diabetes and looked at the effects of lifestyle changes. One group went on just as they had before, receiving no special intervention. The second group underwent a lifestyle and counseling program, receiving help from a dietician every two months for four years. At the end of four years the group that had gone to the lifestyle training had a 58 percent reduction in the development of diabetes. Once again, this proves that it is never too late to make changes![7]

UNACCEPTABLE SUGAR:
PRESSING TOWARD THE GOAL

	UNHEALTHY	IMPROVING	ACHIEVING EXCELLENCE
Daily Sugar Intake	Greater than 150 grams per day*	Between 100 and 150 grams	Less than 100 grams
Fasting Glucose	Greater than 124	Between 100 and 124	Less than 100
C-Peptide	Less than 1.8	Between 1.8 and 3.5	Greater than 3.5
HgbA1c	Less than 5.8	Between 5.8 and 6.4	Greater than 6.4

---

7 J Am Soc Nephrol 14:S108-S113, 2003

* The exact top limit will depend on your goal daily for carbohydrates. To calculate this number take your total calorie goal, multiply by .4 to .5 (40 to 50% of calories from carbohydrates) and divide by 4 (4 calories per gram) to calculate the numbers of grams per day you want to eat. Divide this into 3–6 meals per day (don't forget the liquids—they count too). If this seems too complicated then go see a registered dietitian or doctor to get set up on a plan!

PLAYING THE GAME OF HEALTH

5 STEPS TO ELIMINATING UNACCEPTABLE SUGAR

AWARENESS: Are you aware of your blood sugar level? Do you eat foods that are likely to raise it? How often do you eat bread, pasta, corn, potatoes, rice, cookies, cakes, chips, pies, or ice cream? How much soda or beer do you drink per week? Look in the mirror and assess your body shape; apple or a pear? If you do not know your blood sugar level, find out!

UNDERSTANDING: Are you seeing and grasping the health risks of eating too much sugar? Can you see how many of the carbs you eat affect your body in the same way as sugar? What would motivate you to monitor your sugar intake?

HABITS: What are your top three favorite sugary foods or carbs? Are you reading labels to see how many carbohydrates are in the food you eat? When do you reach for these most? When stressed? When watching TV? Who do you eat them with? How do you feel afterward? Name three things you can do to reduce your sugar intake.

ACCOUNTABILITY: Identify others trying to reduce their sugar intake. Ask them to be an accountability partner. Journal what you eat and share it with them. Consider going to a dietitian and reviewing one week's worth of food choices every month or two. Find healthy food alternatives and share what you find. Look at the carbohydrate content in 10 common foods you eat at the grocery store. Then look for better choices. If you change 3 or 4, you will make a significant change in your life. Share what you learn with a trusted friend and ask them if you can call them anytime you are being tempted to eat something harmful.

SHARING: Write your victories down in your health journal. From time to time, look back and take note of how often you were victorious over your cravings. Reward yourself for a job well done and look for others who are open to learning about Unacceptable Sugars.

NUMBER FIVE

"Two numbers used to describe blood pressure: systolic pressure and diastolic pressure. The systolic pressure, which is always higher and listed first, measures the force that blood exerts on the arterial walls as the heart pumps blood through the body's cardiovascular system. The diastolic pressure, which is always lower and called out second, is the measurement of force as the heart relaxes to allow blood to flow back into the heart. …Blood pressure often decreases when weight decreases, and the greater the weight loss, the greater the reduction in blood pressure."

—*Jordan Rubin*

Jordan Rubin, *Perfect Weight* (Lake Mary, FL: Siloam, A Strang Company, 2008) pp. 208-209.

BLOOD PRESSURE

The **B** in our TROUBLE Assessment stands for *Blood Pressure*. It is the measure of the force at which our blood flows through our arteries. Knowing this number is a major key to knowing if there is any TROUBLE lurking within.

Our blood vessels play a major role in keeping us functioning properly. They make up the transportation system of our body and consist of a series of pipes that carry oxygen, food, messages, and waste products to and from each cell. Every twenty-three seconds, five to six quarts of blood circulate from the heart to the tissues of the body and back. The oxygen, glucose and other nutrients carried in these channels are the lifeblood every cell needs to live. Without these nutrients, our cells would die in a matter of minutes.

Blood vessels are divided into two major categories: the **arterial** system and the **venous** system. Arteries lead *from* the heart to the cells, carrying life-giving oxygen and nutrients. Veins run from the cells back to the heart, returning waste products such as carbon dioxide and acids. The force necessary to push the blood to the cells far exceeds the force needed to return it to the heart. Thus, the walls of the arterial system are much stronger and thicker to withstand the force of each heartbeat.

The force at which the blood flows through the blood vessels is called Blood Pressure. We measure this pressure by wrapping the arm with an inflatable cuff and seeing how much force the heart generates with each beat. The pressure it exerts when it fully contracts is called the *systolic* blood pressure. The pressure it generates when it relaxes is called the *diastolic* blood pressure. The way we express a person's blood pressure is systolic over the diastolic. Blood Pressure (BP) = Systolic pressure/Diastolic pressure = SBP/DBP.

The immediate relaxation of the blood vessels after the heart contracts reinforces the teamwork that occurs between the heart and the blood vessels. This allows blood to flow into the arteries with less resistance. As we age, our arteries become less flexible, and plaque often is deposited in them. This leads to arteries becoming stiff and less able to relax. As this happens, the systolic blood pressure slowly rises. So the increase of plaque and aging of the arteries leads to an increase in blood pressure.

···

The blood vessels are the transportation system of the body. As the heart contracts,

it pushes blood through the arterial system and into the body. Arteries carry

nutrient-rich blood from the heart to the cells of the body. Five to six quarts of

blood circulate from our heart to our cells and back every twenty-three seconds.

···

UNDERSTANDING **THE DANGER OF HIGH BLOOD PRESSURE**

Okay…so what is a healthy, normal blood pressure? It is about 115 systolic over 75 diastolic—115/75. Modern studies have shown that the high elevation of the *top* number and the difference between the top and the bottom number (the pulse pressure) are the best predictors of having a heart attack or stroke in people *over* age 50. On the other hand, the high elevation of the bottom number is the most important predictor for people *under* age 50.

The normal heart rate is 60 to 80 beats per minute. People who have 80 to 120 beats per minute are headed for trouble, and those who are experiencing over 120 beats per minute definitely have a problem. For every 20/10 point increase over the normal pressure of 115/75, the chance of having a heart attack or stroke *doubles*. If my patients have a Blood Pressure under 120/80, I am fine with it. If it is greater than 140 over 90, they have high blood pressure or hypertension and I start treating it with medicine.

When the systolic, or top, number goes up, it causes an increase in the force of blood flow in our tender, sensitive tissues, such as our brain and kidneys. This leads to damage of the blood vessels and/or the tissues themselves. Plaque may begin to build up or the blood vessel wall may thicken or hypertrophy. In the brain, this leads to *multi-infarct dementia,* which means a person has multiple small strokes because of inadequate blood flow to areas of the brain. In the kidneys, this leads to renal failure and eventually the need for dialysis. Overall, an increase in blood pressure results in a decrease in functioning and ultimately death of cells and tissue.

Another potential problem from a weakened arterial wall is that it may stretch and ultimately rip under the increased pressure. This is called an *aneurysm*. One of my patients, an executive for a large Fortune 100 firm, came to my office one day complaining of back pain. I did an exam and found no obvious problem. He had no sign of a pulled muscle or kidney stone and no significant arthritis or stomach problems. But over the course of a few days, the pain worsened. Not wanting to take any chances, we got a CAT scan of his abdomen to see what was going on. When the results came, we had our answer. The largest blood vessel in the body, the aorta, was beginning to tear. Although it was not yet critical, it was only a matter of time before it would have ripped open, and he would have died of internal hemorrhaging. That test saved his life!

The sobering fact about high blood pressure is that it is often without symptoms until it is too late. That is, until an "end organ," such as our brain, kidneys or heart, becomes damaged, we rarely feel it. Occasionally, some individuals with high blood pressure get headaches or blurry vision. But usually they ascribe these symptoms to stress or tension. This is how hypertension got the name "the great silent killer." Many times the first sign that the silent killer has invaded our body is when we experience kidney failure, an aneurysm, a stroke or a heart attack.

One of my greatest goals in life is to help people avoid this type of irreversible damage and live the healthy life we were meant to live. Some causes of hypertension are preventable and can be reversed. Certain tumors, kidney problems and heart conditions that lead to blood pressure elevations are correctable once we discover and address the root cause. Therefore, have your doctor look for these other conditions, checking them out with your blood work and any other tests they feel are necessary to reveal these reversible symptoms.

*For every 20/10 point increase over the normal pressure of 115/75, the chance of having a heart attack or stroke **doubles**. If you have high blood pressure, do not ignore it! Hypertension is often called "the great silent killer" because many people often do not feel any pain until it kills them suddenly.*

HOW **SALT EFFECTS BLOOD PRESSURE**

In Texas, we understand the meaning of summer heat. Temperatures often soar over 100, and experiencing days or weeks without rain are not unusual. On hot, sticky nights, all we want is something refreshing to help us cool down and forget the sweltering heat. Some may think, what better summer night drink than a margarita? Well, that is not necessarily the case.

Unfortunately, the amount of salt in a margarita is high. As it is taken in, sodium quickly flows into the bloodstream. To deal with this dilemma, our kidneys retain water to dilute the salt content. Our kidneys are the volume controllers of our blood. Whether it is a margarita or another salt-satu-rated food, our kidneys are designed to maintain healthy blood-salt con-tent. Having too much sodium in the blood is called *hypernatremia*. This condition leads to mental confusion, heart problems and death to cells.

Most individuals can tolerate an increased amount of sodium from one food item without difficulties. Our blood vessels usually operate half filled. So to accommodate the situation, they just relax and allow the increased volume to work its way through the system, allowing the kidneys to catch up and process the excess salt load. As we age, however, our body's ability to handle excessive amounts of salt diminishes. Our arteries and kidneys don't always work as well as they did when we were younger. They may be able to handle the surplus salt from *one* food item, but any additional salty foods will tip the scales.

Salty foods are often eaten in concert with others. For example, if we are eating a Mexican meal, salsa, chips, enchiladas, and sopapillas are often eaten together—all of which contain copious amounts of salt. If we're eating our favorite combo, the burger, fries and soda are also filled with sodium, not to mention a lot of fat. Excessive amounts of salt in the blood stream cause the blood pressure to rise dramatically. Unfortunately, the body has no warning system for this, so we usually don't feel any symptoms. If we do have symptoms, we often ascribe them to other ingredients in our food or to being tired. Consequently, the real problem goes unnoticed.

High blood pressure resulting from an excessive amount of salt in our diet is a phenomenon that occurs frequently in modern society. As mentioned earlier, almost all of our processed foods contain moderate to large amounts of salt. From potato chips and hot dogs to canned soup and macaroni and cheese, salt is added to enhance flavor and preserve shelf life. We must develop a healthy habit of reading food labels.

For example, check out the food label for a popular processed cheese. As you can see, it packs quite a punch in several areas. It has a high amount of saturated fat—74 of the 101 calories are from fat. It also contains 443 mg of sodium, which is about 25 percent of the daily recommended salt intake. Remember, we want our daily consumption of fat to remain below 30 percent of our total calories, and the amount of salt we consume should be less than 2 grams (2,000 mg). I am *not* saying you can never eat a slice of this cheese. What I am saying is be aware of what you are eating so that you don't overload your system with too much salt or fat. An ounce of prevention is worth a pound of cure.

....

Excessive amounts of salt in the bloodstream cause our blood pressure to rise dramatically. Our daily consumption of salt should be less than 2 grams (2,000 mg). To know how much sodium you are taking in, read the food labels.

....

WHAT ABOUT **WEIGHT GAIN**?

Cheese American, Swiss, Processed | Nutrition Facts

Serving Size: 1 oz, Land O' Lakes

Serving Per Container

Amount Per Serving		
Calories 101	Calories from Fat 74	
	% Daily Value	
Total Fat 8.3 g		0%
Saturated Fat 5.2 g		0%
Monosaturated fat 2.2 g		
Polynsaturated Fat 0.3 g		
Cholesterol 26 mg		
Sodium 443 mg		
Total Carbohydrate 0.7 g		
Dietary Fiber 0 g		
Sugars 0 g		
Protein 5.8 g		

Our blood pressure will also increase as a result of weight gain. There are a number of reasons this occurs. One of the most eye-opening is that our body creates and lays down new blood vessels at the same time our fat cells pack away fat. For every pound of fat we gain, our body manufactures and lays down an additional *mile* of blood vessels and then pump blood the increased distance to keep the tissues alive. Wow!

So, if a person is 30 pounds overweight, they have approximately 30 extra miles of blood vessels to create and pump blood through. Excess weight also makes the heart work harder, which translates to more beats per minute. There are 60 minutes in an hour and 24 hours in a day. If this person's heart beats 80 times a minute, his heart will beat about 115,200 beats a day—that is 80 x 60 x 24. What's more, his heart will have to pump blood an additional 3,456,000 *miles per day! Do the math:* 80 x 60 x 24 x 30 miles.

Current statistics estimate that over two-thirds of all Americans are overweight, a number of which are morbidly obese. There is little wonder why epidemics of both hypertension and congestive heart failure are currently appearing in our country today. It's high time we get into the game and start calling some different plays.

Our body creates and lays down new blood vessels at the same time our fat cells pack away fat. For every pound of fat we gain, our body has to manufacture an additional mile of blood vessels and then pump blood the increased distance to keep the tissues alive.

HOW **SALT EFFECTS BLOOD PRESSURE**

As a first-year medical student, I arrived convinced that modern medicine had all the answers. I believed I was in for the educational experience of a lifetime. When we started pathophysiology, I just knew the teachers were speaking the "gospel" truth regarding the human body. Likewise, with regard to cardiovascular disease, such as strokes, heart attacks, and aneurysms, I was very sure that we in the medical profession had it all figured out. Smoking, diabetes, high blood pressure, elevated cholesterol, lack of exercise, estrogen deficiency, and family history are all factors that lead to a weakened and broken heart…or so I believed.

At some point in my journey I remember wondering: What on earth do these seven things have in common? Why do a lack of estrogen and exercise have the same effect as diabetes and smoking? At that time, I was told that these factors led to a gradual blockage of the blood vessels by an accumulation of plaque—the process known as atherosclerosis. When the opening in the artery became too small for blood to flow through it, a blood clot formed. Any tissues downstream from this clot died, and the person with such a condition would experience a heart attack, stroke or another unexpected, catastrophic event.

While all these things are true to an extent, there are other factors involved that the medical profession was unaware of at the time. The truth is, medical information and understanding doubles about every two years. We are constantly learning new things. What we think is correct today will be modified in the years ahead as our knowledge increases.

119

One powerful factor determining the health of the heart and the circulatory system we were not aware of in the 1980s is the key role the *vascular endothelium* plays. This thin, one-cell-layer lining of our blood vessels is a pivotal part of the health of our entire body. It was overlooked for decades in the medical field, apparently because of its thinness and suspected frailty. Nevertheless, this seemingly insignificant lining is the largest endocrine gland in the human body!

Altogether it weighs over 1.6 pounds in the average adult male. If we took our skin off and made it into a carpet (strange thought, but stay with me), it would be three feet by three feet square. However, if we took the lining of all our blood vessels and put it together, the vascular endothelium would measure three *football fields* in size! This amazing, microscopic layer sets the stage for health or disease. If it is healthy, the body is positioned to be healthy. If it is damaged, the door is open for disease to develop.

· ·

*The **vascular endothelium**, the inner lining of all our blood vessels, is the largest endocrine gland in the human body. This seemingly insignificant layer sets the stage for health or disease within the body. If it is healthy, the body is positioned to be healthy. If it is damaged, the door is open for disease to develop.*

· ·

WHAT HAPPENS **WHEN THE LINING GETS DAMAGED**?

One of the most common initial irritants to the lining of the blood vessels is the persistent presence of insulin. As we learned earlier, when digested food is making its way through the small intestines, the pancreas releases the hormone insulin. Insulin serves as a messenger that signals the cells of the body to open their doors and let the "food" in. The more sugar and fat we eat, the more insulin is needed to tell the cells to take it in. When the cells are full, excess sugar and fat remain in the blood. This causes the pancreas to produce and release more insulin. Eventually the cells become resistant to insulin, giving way to the *insulin resistance syndrome* (IRS) that we have discussed earlier in this book. This is also known as *metabetes*—the name describing this pre-diabetic condition.

When metabetes moves into the neighborhood, our vascular endothelial lining begins experiencing significant stress. Once it is damaged, a chain reaction of destruction begins. The lining begins to react by sending up "warning flags" called ICAMs (intracellular adhesion molecules) or VCAMs (vascular adhesion molecules). These fighter molecules sound an alarm for the "law enforcement" of the body to come and make repairs to the damaged lining.

The "law" arrives in the form of molecules called macrophages. Their job is to absorb the excess LDL, or lethal cholesterol, and protect the blood vessel from plaque formation. However, because there is not enough room in the blood vessel for both the macrophage and LDL molecules, further irritation occurs. This releases more ICAMs and VCAMS that call for help. More macrophages come to the scene and another battle ensues. This vicious cycle of irritation or inflammation with the LDL molecules and the macrophage cells causes the wall of the artery to become "hot" from the conflict.

From here, one of two things will happen. The body will get relief from the fight because we get up and start exercising and making changes to our eating habits or we begin to take cholesterol- lowering medication. If these positive adjustments are not made, a life-threatening consequence will ensue. The combination of LDL and macrophage molecules become intertwined and burrowed into the artery wall as "foam cells," the primary ingredient in plaque. This plaque may become unstable and rupture into the bloodstream. This results in "exploding plaque," the underlying cause of both heart attacks and strokes.

Other things that damage the lining of blood vessels include high blood pressure, diabetes, smoking, a persistent amount of emotional stress or depression, and excess fat/cholesterol in the blood. Sadly, any one of these problems by themselves is dangerous. However, when two or more are present working together, they become a lethal wrecking crew. Instead of just attacking one area of the body, they bring destruction to multiple areas— attacking arteries in places like the legs, kidneys, neck, and head simultaneously. The only thing worse than being in trouble with the "IRS" (having Insulin Resistance Syndrome) is being in TROUBLE and not being able to do anything about it.

· ·

High blood pressure, diabetes, smoking, persistent amounts of insulin or emotional stress hormones in the bloodstream, and excess fat/cholesterol in the blood damage the lining of blood vessels. Sadly, any one of these problems by themselves is dangerous. However, when two or more are present working together, they become a lethal wrecking crew.

· ·

THE **THREADBARE TIRE PRINCIPLE**

As a student at Tampa General Hospital, I spent a lot of time in the medicine wards and in the emergency room. One month, while working in the ER, a very nice, older African-American patient, who I'll call "Henry," came in with a prostate problem. While treating him, I noticed his blood pressure was high. I asked him if he had ever been told this. He looked at his wife and daughter who were in the room and chuckled, "Yes, they tell me that, but I never had any trouble with it, so I don't treat it." I insisted on writing him a prescription for high blood pressure medicine and asked his family to make sure he took it. People of all ethnicities have an increase in blood pressure as they age. But African-Americans have a greater risk. In fact, by the time African-American women are 80 years old, 80 percent of them have blood pressures of over 140/90.

Several months later, when I was on the intensive care unit (ICU) rotation, Henry came back to the hospital, only this time it was because of a stroke. Because I had seen him and had a relationship with his family, the resident doctor asked me to monitor the case personally through the night.

That was one of the most devastating nights of my life. We tried to control Henry's blood pressure with intravenous drips. Unfortunately, part of his brain was not getting blood, and it was dying. The part of his body it controlled was moving uncontrollably. About halfway through the night, his brain began to swell and push its way through the opening in his supporting tissue inside the skull. His arms and legs then stretched out and assumed a position we call decorticate posturing. Soon afterward, he began to have seizures, and finally, he died. His wife just kept crying and saying, "He never would take his medicine." I did my best to ease her conscience, but we both knew this could have been prevented.

As a doctor, one of the most frustrating things to deal with is a patient who refuses to take his/her medicine. Years ago, when I diagnosed my patients with high cholesterol, I would immediately ask them to begin therapy. However, only four out of ten would agree to it. When asked why, they often responded, "I feel just fine. It can't be that big of a deal."

I tried to politely explain the seriousness of their situation, but it rarely did any good. Finally, in my desperation to wake people up, I began saying, "It doesn't matter how you feel. This condition will still kill you." This increased my success rate somewhat, but it still wasn't what it should be. And a number of my patients mistook my sense of urgency for rudeness and insensitivity. So I began to use the following analogy:

A man pulled off a highway into a filling station to fuel up his pristine 1970 Ford pickup. The attendant saw him pull in and struck up a conversation.

"Nice old truck you've got there," the attendant commented.

"Yup," replied the man proudly, "I been driving it for a lot of years."

As they spoke the attendant noticed the tires were all completely bald.

"Uh...change your tires recently?" he asked with raised eyebrows.

"Nope, never. And do ya know what? I've got over 100,000 miles on this truck, and it drives great and ain't never had a flat."

At this point, more of my patients began to get the idea. My success rate of getting them to take their medication and do therapy increased to about seven out of ten. I guess the others will have to experience a "blowout" to take it seriously. Hopefully you are not one of them. It takes a mature person to feel fine, yet pay money for medication, doctor visits, lab tests, and deal with the inconvenience of it all based upon someone encouraging them to do it. Hopefully, as you play the Game of Health and understand what is actually happening in your body, the motivation to stay in the Game and win will become easier and more likely to occur.

· ·

People of all ethnicities have an increase in blood pressure as they age. But African-Americans have a greater risk. In fact, by the time African-American women are 80 years old, 80 percent of them have blood pressures of over 140/90.

· ·

IT'S TIME TO **TAKE ACTION NOW**!

So what is your *Blood Pressure*? If you don't know, it is time to find out. If you *do* know your blood pressure and it is higher than it should be, there is no time like the present to take action. The same is true if you have elevated Oil or Unacceptable Sugar levels.

The "Eight Report of the Joint National Committee on Prevention, Detection, Evaluation, and Treatment of High Blood Pressure" provides guidelines for hypertension prevention and management. Here are its key findings:

> In people **over 50**, *systolic blood pressure* greater than 140 mmHg is a much more important cardiovascular disease (CVD) risk factor than diastolic blood pressure.
>
> The risk of developing CVD doubles with each increment of 20/10 mmHg beyond the healthy pressure of 115/75 mmHg. Individuals who have a normal blood pressure at age 55 have a *90 percent* lifetime risk for developing hypertension.
>
> Individuals with a systolic blood pressure of 120–139 mmHg or a diastolic blood pressure of 80–89 mmHg should be considered pre-hypertensive and require health-promoting lifestyle modifications to prevent the development of heart attacks and strokes.[8]

Without a doubt, the human body is incredibly created and very accommodating. It's always trying to adapt and adjust to whatever we eat, drink and do. It will bend over backwards to keep us functioning properly. So take some time to learn more about your body and give it what it needs. By lowering your blood pressure through increased exercise, salt restriction, and medication if need be, you can get your numbers where they need to

---

7 J Am Soc Nephrol 14:S108-S113, 2003

be and maximize your chances of avoiding "stiff vessels" and reverse the process of plaque buildup, and in many cases, prevent the progression into irreversible consequences. Get with your healthcare provider. See where you are in the Game, and team up to send hypertension back to its bench. Yes, it may require some effort and be a bit inconvenient, but it will make a big difference in the quality and length of your life.

BLOOD PRESSURE: PRESSING TOWARD THE GOAL

	UNHEALTHY	IMPROVING	ACHIEVING EXCELLENCE
Systolic	Greater than 140	Between 120 to 140	Less than 120
Diastolic	Greater than 90	Between 80 to 90	Less than 80

PLAYING THE GAME OF HEALTH

5 STEPS TO IMPROVING YOUR BLOOD PRESSURE

AWARENESS: What is your blood pressure? Is it normal, borderline, or high? Is it where you would like it to be? Are you in TROUBLE?

UNDERSTANDING: From this chapter, can you see the chain reaction of problems that arise as a result of high blood pressure? Do you see how not dealing with it will eventually not only affect you but those whom you love? What steps can you take to either lower your blood pressure if it's high or maintain a healthy blood pressure?

HABITS: Blood pressure can be greatly affected by sodium (salt) intake, your level of fitness (especially aerobic fitness) and your weight. Are you in the habit of looking at labels to check the salt content? Do you get your heart rate to your goal level for at least 20 minutes 3 times weekly? Is your BMI at goal? What habits are keeping these three keys from getting to goal?

ACCOUNTABILITY: Who prepares your food? Can you team up with them to cut sodium? How about aerobic exercise? Who could you ask to work out with you and help you stay in shape? Is there a group at church, work or school that may be helpful to keep you on track? What is your goal? Who can you declare it to and have them ask you regularly if you are meeting it? It takes a village to live a great life. Don't try to do it alone!

SHARING: As you become more and more disciplined in your training and eating regimen, record your blood pressure every time you have it taken. Write it down in your journal. Look back after a few months and see how much you've been able to lower it. Reward yourself for sticking to your plan and getting healthy! Do something you have wanted to do for a long time but have not gotten around to. Who can you share this life-changing information with?

127

NUMBER SIX

"Every year in the U.S. over 392,000 people die from tobacco-caused disease, making it the leading cause of preventable death. Another 50,000 people die from exposure to secondhand smoke. Tragically, each day thousands of kids still pick up a cigarette for the first time. The cycle of addiction, illness and death continues. ...Quitting smoking is the single most important step a smoker can take to improve the length and quality of his or her life."

—*American Lung Association*

Retrieved 5/18/11 (http://www.lungusa.org/stop-smoking/ and http://www.lungusa.org/stop-smoking/how-to-quit/getting-help/).

LOUSY HABITS

The **L** in our TROUBLE Assessment stands for *Lousy Habits*. A habit is a behavior pattern developed by frequent repetition. It is closely connected with both the way we think and how we feel emotionally. *Lousy Habits* rob us of a quality life and in some cases, shorten our years. They compound the negative effects of unhealthy food choices, increased Roundness and a lack of Training in our lives.

There are countless Lousy Habits we can develop, ranging from taking drugs and drinking excessive amounts of alcohol to watching too much TV and not getting enough sleep. But there is one Lousy Habit I want to zero in on—one that has impacted the lives of almost all of us directly or indirectly. That is the Lousy Habit of *smoking*.

THE **DESTRUCTIVE PROPERTIES OF CIGARETTES**

What do you think of when you see a cigarette? Picture this: Tobacco seeds are planted and the ground is fertilized with chemicals. As the plants grow, they are sprayed with pesticides. Once tobacco leaves fully mature, they are picked and transported to a factory where they are soaked in preservatives and other flavorings. They are then packaged into neat, small cigarettes for distribution. We now know that addictive-forming ingredients are added to cigarettes. This means the entire manufacturing process is carefully manipulated to insure that the smoker's "experience" is carefully controlled and keeps them coming back for more.

All of us have heard of the straw that broke the camel's back. Well, tobacco is the match that ignites the fire inside a person's blood vessels. This is especially true when they already have their hands full dealing with the "IRS"—Insulin Resistance Syndrome, or metabetes. In this condition, smoking irritates the "silver lining" of our blood vessels, the vascular endothelium, even more. As a result, its healthy functioning declines even further.

When a person lights up and inhales, all that was put into making the cigarette is breathed into the lungs. I call these the "products of ignition." They include the fertilizers, pesticides, preservatives, flavorings, burned paper, and of course, nicotine. There are actually over 200 different chemicals found in cigarettes, including arsenic, carbon monoxide, miscellaneous hydrocarbons, and other free radicals and toxins. All of these are heated to red-hot temperatures, inhaled into the lungs, transferred to the blood and dispersed throughout the body.

Smoking unleashes an attack of literally tens of thousands of destructive energy particles within the body. As they make their way through the bloodstream, dangerous free radicals strike and injure the walls of the arteries. These new open wounds become gaps for lethal LDL cholesterol to sneak in and lodge within the blood vessel wall. The inflammation and irritation LDL brings leads to a damaged artery, which is the first step in the accumulation of plaque, which we will see in the next chapter.

Sadly, each cigarette will take five to seven minutes off a smoker's life. Death comes an average of 15 years earlier for a smoker than a non-smoker. Clearly, lighting up is a Lousy Habit that leaves a lousy legacy for generations to come.

....

Addiction-forming ingredients are added to cigarettes. Over 200 different chemicals are found in them, including arsenic, carbon monoxide, hydrocarbons, and other free radicals and toxins. Each cigarette will take five to seven minutes off a smoker's life. Death comes an average of 15 years earlier for a smoker than a non-smoker.

....

MY EXPERIENCE **WORKING WITH SMOKERS**

The use of cigarettes and other nicotine-based products is one of the most perplexing trends we have in the U.S. today. As a medical student at the Tampa Veterans Administration Hospital, I saw the tragic result of our government's discount cigarette program manifested in former soldiers day after day, literally by the hundreds. The story always ends the same. Veterans developed lung cancer, chronic obstructive pulmonary disease (COPD), suffocation from emphysema or plaque formation resulting in a stroke, aneurysm, or heart attack.

As a young, enthusiastic student of the healing arts, it was incomprehensible to me that people could so knowingly kill themselves through smoking. I can remember becoming boiling angry at the patients as they suffered from what I felt was self-induced agony. And God forbid if they complained, because I didn't want to hear it! I simply had no tolerance. At that time I had no *understanding* of the nature of the addiction they suffered from. It just seemed they were reaping what they had sown. I remember saying with great bravado as a first-year med student, "I will not see smokers in *my* practice when I graduate."

The thing that eventually saved me from my ignorance and arrogance was my love of history. As a child, I was a member of the military book club. Yeah, I was a nerd. Nevertheless, I read all of the books by Edward L. Beach, like *Run Silent Run Deep*, and *The Two Ocean War: A Short History of the U.S. Navy in the Second World War* by Samuel Eliot Morison. I basically knew World War II in terms of the battles—what happened and who won.

This love of history peaked during those all-nighters when I was on call in the Veterans Administration Hospital. I often sat in the ward, monitoring patients and conversing with veterans about their war experiences. Several of these men had fought on the beaches of the Pacific Ocean. Some had even been on submarines and survived being sunk! Others were pilots who fought in the European theater, the Pacific theater, or both. The more I talked with them, the more I learned that they were not "bad," irresponsible men. They were the backbone of our military doing their best to protect our freedom during the Second World War.

Forty-three years after the last shots of the war had been fired, they were still experiencing the ravages of battle. The only difference was that the enemy no longer had a face, and death no longer came in the form of gunshots or bomb blasts. These men were now experiencing the consequences of serving in a very scary war—one in which they were not sure if they would live another day. To help the men cope with the stresses of war, our government had provided free and discount cigarettes. Many men shared with amazement their memories of being able to go to the base to buy packs of cigarettes for twenty-five cents.

Cigarette programs were not a malicious or careless act. They were primarily a decision made without the proper medical knowledge. It wasn't until many years after the war that the dangers of smoking were realized. By the mid-1980s, we better understood the destructive nature of cigarettes and that they were killing thousands of our veterans. By then, many veterans and common folk alike had a serious addiction that they could not figure out how to break free from. For many, it was too late to receive much benefit from stopping.

Separating the person from the disease was a hard lesson to learn. It was one of those rights of passage for me as a medical student. Initially, I attempted to assign an explanation to each person for every medical problem they had. I wanted to make them admit that *they* had brought the problems onto themselves. This way I could feel confident that if I did the right things in my own life, I would never experience the same problems. Those long nights on call in the ward did a lot more than teach me medicine. They taught me about life and helped me understand that bad things *do* happen to good people.

. . . .

For U.S. veterans and common folk alike, smoking cigarettes always creates

the same kind of results: lung cancer, chronic obstructive pulmonary disease

(COPD), suffocation from emphysema or a stroke, aneurysm or a heart attack.

. . . .

UNDERSTANDING **HOW ADDICTION TAKES ROOT**

To understand how a person becomes addicted to smoking, we must first understand a few things about nicotine and the human body. Nicotine is a *neurotransmitter*. It is a normal, healthy, important molecule that transmits nerve impulses and messages from one nerve to the next. It is associated with a part of the nervous system that's involved with alertness and focus. The interesting thing is, our body produces nicotine all by itself.

So here we have our poor, unsuspecting young soldier, who we'll call "George." Not knowing if he's going to see the next sunrise, he is offered the "pleasure" of discount cigarettes. He begins smoking, and within a short time, becomes addicted to the nicotine delivery device. If we tested George before and after he smoked, we'd find his test-taking ability was better *after* smoking his cigarette than before.

After George smokes for a few weeks, his body realizes that it no longer needs to make its own nicotine because of the seemingly endless supply of it flowing into the bloodstream from an unknown source. His body then proceeds to tear down its nicotine-producing factories. If George quits smoking, his focus and test-taking abilities will temporarily sink below the level they were before he started smoking. *He has to smoke to get back to his baseline functioning.*

. . . .

Nicotine is a normal, healthy neurotransmitter—an important molecule that transmits messages from one nerve to the next. It is associated with a part of the nervous system that's involved with alertness and focus. The interesting thing is, our body produces nicotine all by itself.

. . . .

From this point forward, if George doesn't get his military ration of cigarettes, he will go through physical withdrawals from the absence of nicotine. His body's nervous system needs to send messages, but without its nicotine factories or the external provision of nicotine from smoking, it is unable to do so. It will take at least three days to rebuild its internal factories. During this time George will be irritable, feel jittery, suffer from insomnia and perhaps develop a rapid heartbeat and sweating. He will want a cigarette so desperately that he will go through the ritual of seeking one out. He is now addicted to the neurotransmitter delivery device we know as cigarettes.

Another controlling factor that comes with cigarette smoking is the perceived relaxation it brings. Think about it. When George needs to smoke, he gets up, strolls over to a quiet place, lights up a cigarette and reflects on his day. Unconsciously, he has done a good thing by taking a moment to relax. Unfortunately, he has now attached smoking to relaxation. Now whenever he feels irritable or stressed for any reason, he heads off for a cigarette to calm his nerves. He has established smoking as a way of coping with stress.

In a short time, smoking becomes a *reflex*. If the phone rings, George grabs a cigarette. When he gets into the car to drive to work, he grabs a cigarette. When he gets out of the shower, finishes dinner, goes for a walk, and so forth, he grabs a cigarette. Eventually, lighting up is second nature and requires no thought on his part whatsoever. He has acquired a deeply seated Lousy Habit.

Not all of us are equally susceptible to the addictive power of cigarettes or other tobacco products. This fact becomes especially pronounced when we take a look in the psychiatric wards of hospitals. Seemingly every psychotic person craves cigarettes, as do many of those with a manic-depressive illness. On the other hand, those with obsessive-compulsive disorders and anxiety disorders smoke far less. It has become evident that those individuals who have a psychiatric disorder involving low dopamine levels are more prone to smoke. Consequently, it will be more difficult for them to quit.

....

If a person quits smoking, it will take at least three days for their body to rebuild its internal nicotine factories. During this time, he will be irritable, feel jittery, suffer from insomnia and perhaps develop a rapid heartbeat and sweating.

....

TAKING THE **STEPS TO WALK IN FREEDOM**

Thankfully, there are successful ways to quit smoking. Through commitment, perseverance and a good plan, it can be done! To be effective, the plan must address each of the issues mentioned in the previous section. Let's take a look at a proven plan of action based on the five points in the Game of Health.

The first step to freedom is honestly becoming **aware** of your condition. Ask yourself, *Do I have a problem with nicotine? Am I addicted?* If you are and you admit it, you have moved out of the Dugout of Life and are in position to begin making your way around the bases.

Your next step is **understanding**, which means learning about tobacco's effects on your body and the importance of moving beyond the addiction. We already mentioned a number of effects tobacco has, but you can learn even more through the additional resources we have made available online at **www.mysevenhealers.com**.

The greatest key to freedom is dealing with the pure physical addiction to nicotine. Again, the body must have nicotine in order to function. Weaning oneself of smoking in steps through "nicotine replacement therapy" is a proven remedy. This includes the use of nicotine gums, patches or delivery devices like smokeless cigarettes. You may ask, "Well, isn't that just as bad?" In a sense, it is similar to smoking in that it continues to supply nicotine externally. However, it does not deliver the other toxins associated with lighting a cigarette, and the doses of nicotine are carefully controlled and systematically reduced to slowly wean a person off external sources. For instance, nicotine patches can be reduced from 21 mg to 14 mg to 7 mg before eliminating it completely.

If a person chooses to stop smoking cold turkey, their body will rebuild its nicotine factories and begin producing nicotine again after about 72 hours. This period will be more than a little difficult, but some would rather tough it out as opposed to gradually tapering off over days, weeks, or months with gum, patches or smokeless forms of nicotine.

....

The greatest key to freedom from smoking is dealing with the physical addiction to nicotine. Weaning oneself in steps through "nicotine replacement therapy" is a proven remedy. This includes the use of nicotine gums, patches or delivery devices like smokeless cigarettes.

....

New ways of managing stress will also be needed to quit. The relaxing break that smoking provides—standing up, walking outside, talking with friends, and taking a few deep breaths is a good form of therapy. To suddenly stop these things can lead to a return to smoking. Harnessing the good habits and eliminating the Lousy Habit of smoking is the key. Stress-Maps is a tool I use to help patients identify and address the areas of their life in which they are struggling and provide them with tools to overcome them. You can check out StressMaps at **www.thesevennumbers.com**.

Once you are aware of where you are and have a better understanding of your situation, it is time to develop **new habits**. Experts estimate it takes about 21 days to establish these. New, healthier patterns of behavior will help prevent an inadvertent return to smoking. Some successful habits to consider include wearing a rubber band and flicking it when the urge to smoke returns. Deep-breathing exercises and counting backward from 10 may also be helpful.

I have worked with many people who have quit smoking, and it appears that with each unhealthy habit they have had, they had to "say no" to it *three* times before it was "extinguished." Therefore, if the average person has about 50 different cues to smoke, we will need to say NO about 150 times. Everyday activities such as showering, driving, eating, having sex, and experiencing stressful situations are often triggers to light up. If any of these are triggers for you, you will have to recognize them and guard yourself to do one of the proactive "antidotes" like deep breathing, the rubber band, or some other refocusing technique to move past these cues.

The second to last step in our trip around the bases is establishing **accountability**. Finding trustworthy people who will support us in our endeavors is a major key to victory. Stop and think. Who can be recruited to help you quit smoking? Friends, family members and coworkers can be great accountability partners during the challenging transition. When my dad wanted to kick the habit back in the 60s, my sister and I gladly agreed to act as protagonists in the effort. The key is to find someone who you talk with or see regularly who won't condemn you for falling off the wagon but at the same time won't condone it either.

Sharing is the final step. Once you have gotten the upper hand in the situation, it is time to begin telling others about your success and offer them help with their struggles. They may ask you questions you don't know the answers to, and that's okay. You can simply refer back to your research sources online or in books and find the answer they need. You may also come up with a completely different way to manage the problem—an idea they had not thought of! By being real, transparent, and willing to help others, you will develop a greater level of freedom than you ever thought possible!

....

New ways of managing stress will also be needed to quit smoking. This means developing new, healthy habits and saying "no" to the old ones. It appears that with each unhealthy habit you have, you will have to say no to it three times before it is "extinguished."

....

Don't Let Lousy Habits Master You!

There is a powerful saying written about 2,000 years ago, and I believe it is very true. It says, "Everything is permissible (allowable and lawful) for me; but not all things are helpful (good for me to do, expedient and profitable when considered with other things). Everything is lawful for me, but *I will not become the slave of anything* or be brought under its power" (1 Corinthians 6:12 AMP). A Lousy Habit, like smoking, may be permissible, but it is definitely *not* helpful or profitable when considered with other things. In most cases it does enslave the person who practices it.

Don't let *Lousy Habits* master you or rob you of a desirable, quality life. If cigarette smoking is a problem, make a solid decision to break free from it. If it's watching too much TV or not getting enough sleep, develop a plan of action to break free. Consult your doctor and seek help from trusted friends.

Only by acknowledging the problem and addressing it will you truly be free. Don't believe the lie that you can't do it. YOU CAN! You can do anything if you put your heart and mind into it. Live your life one day at a time and look for ways to establish healthy habits. Not only will *you* reap the reward of your choices, but your children and your children's children will too!

LOUSY HABITS:
PRESSING TOWARD THE GOAL

HABITS	UNHEALTHY	IMPROVING	ACHIEVING EXCELLENCE
Smoking/ Tobacco Use	Yes	Reducing amount used	None
Hours of TV Per Week	20 or more	15 to 20	Less than 15
Hours of Sleep per Week	Less than 49	49 to 54	Greater than 54

PLAYING THE GAME OF HEALTH

5 STEPS TO ELIMINATING THE LOUSY HABIT OF SMOKING

AWARENESS: Do you smoke? If the answer is yes, how often do you smoke and how long have you been smoking?

UNDERSTANDING: Do you understand the deadly effects that smoking has on your body? Although it is hard to quit, can you see why it is vital that you try? Take a piece of paper and draw a line down the center of it. On one side of the line, list some reasons why you'd like to quit smoking. On the other side, list reasons why you don't want to quit. Does the column listing the reasons you want to quit outweigh the column listing the reasons you want to smoke?

HABITS: What habits in your daily routine motivate you to light up? In what practical ways can you change the way you respond to the stimulus to smoke—what healthy habits can you develop to help you relax and deal with stress in a constructive way?

ACCOUNTABILITY: To whom can you be accountable to help you quit smoking? Ask them to ask you how you are doing on a regular basis. Also, check with your doctor to see if he has any resources that will help you in your effort to quit. You may also want to consider joining a support group or coaching program if there is one available.

SHARING: Take time daily to read your list of reasons to quit smoking. Remind yourself regularly why you are giving it up. Record your struggles and triumphs in your health journal. Look over it from time to time to see how much you grow throughout the process. As you gain victory over the urge, look for opportunities to share your story with others.

NUMBER SEVEN

"...Imagine your arteries as being like streets in a city. We use the streets of a city to get from place to place. Similarly, your blood uses the arteries as a means to get from one place to another. It uses the vessels to carry nutrients and oxygen to the cells, and then carry carbon dioxide and other by-products of metabolism away from the cells. But the arteries, just like streets and highways, eventually wear down. They become clogged with fatty buildup called plaque, or narrowed from swelling and inflammation.... The older and more congested arteries get, the more subject they are to blood clots, the body's version of traffic jams."

—*Michael F. Roizen, M.D.*

Michael F. Roizen, M.D., The RealAge Makeover (New York, NY: HarperCollins Publishers, 2004) p. 93.

EXPLODING PLAQUE

The **E** in our TROUBLE Assessment stands for *Exploding Plaque*. Throughout our journey, I have talked about plaque formation and the problems it brings. In this final section, we want to take a closer look at the reality of what happens to men and women when plaque builds up in the arteries and then ruptures without warning.

UNDERSTANDING **HOW THE BODY RESPONDS TO PLAQUE**

The metabolic war within the bloodstream eventually moves into the walls of our arteries if left unchecked. The lining of the blood vessel, or vascular endothelium, then quits functioning normally. This enables, or encourages, LDL (lousy, lethal cholesterol) and macrophage molecules to invade the wall and pour fuel on an intensifying, fiery battle. As the fight continues, plaque grows. This increases the likelihood of it rupturing and spilling its fatty gel into the bloodstream.

The body, sensing the impending TROUBLE, sends in special "troops" to fight and protect the bloodstream from exposure to the fatty gel and an almost certain blockage of the artery. These troops are *smooth muscle cells*. They arrive at the place of instability in the lining and line up next to each other. They then begin to produce fibrin and collagen, which are the bricks and mortar needed to build a wall of protection against the unstable plaque.

In some cases, smooth muscle cells are able to form a cap over the plaque, and the danger of an explosion diminishes. Eventually the situation stabilizes and the immediate danger passes. Often this area becomes completely secure, no longer in danger of causing an emergency. Sometimes the scar that the smooth cells formed blocks the artery. If this happens, when we use these muscles more, such as in exercising, the tissue downstream from this area may become starved for oxygen, causing us to experience some pain called angina. If this plaque buildup occurs in the blood vessels in the legs, it is called *peripheral vascular disease*. The pain will pass with time if the stress is reduced.

In other cases, the troops are not able to stabilize the area in time. Despite their efforts, the macrophages and the smooth muscle cells cannot overcome the inflammation and irritation in the artery lining. As a result, the wall containing the plaque rips open, and the blood is suddenly exposed to the fatty gel. At this moment, the blood cells take action and immediately form a blood clot over the area. If the person is taking aspirin regularly, the blood clot formed will be less voracious, large, and "sticky." However, if the person uses tobacco, the clot will be thicker and more likely to block the whole artery, causing major problems.

....

As plaque grows, it increases the likelihood of it breaking open and spilling its toxic, fatty gel into the blood. The body sends smooth muscle cells to the inflamed area to build a protective wall of fibrin and collagen. If fibrin and collagen can form a cap or scar over the area effectively, the risk of the exploding plaque will diminish. If not, a blood clot will likely form.

....

IDENTIFYING THE **SYMPTOMS OF A RUPTURED ARTERY**

For many, if not most, of the people who experience the rupture just described, it happens unexpectedly. Most of them are going about their normal, daily business and suddenly become aware of a change in their body. It may start off as a small tickle or irritation. It may feel like tightness in the chest. Or the pain may hit them suddenly, like a baseball bat slamming against their upper body. Other symptoms that may be felt include nausea, sweating, or shortness of breath. In medical school we were taught that any pain between the chin and the belly button is a heart attack until proven otherwise. I dread this day for the many people I care for who are at increased risk of plaque formation.

If the blood vessel experiencing this trauma is in the brain, a *stroke* occurs. If it is in a small non-vital vessel, there may be no sign of a problem at all. If the rupture occurs in a stomach vessel, a severe stomach-ache may accompany it. If it takes place in the legs, leg cramps usually follow, or one or two toes may turn black or purple. If the rupture occurs closer to the carotid artery in the neck, the effects may be devastating, resulting in paralysis of a part to half of the body. If plaque explodes in the heart, a *heart attack* occurs—a tragic event that takes place every thirty seconds in America, as it did in my mentor friend who went for a jog and never returned.

. . . .

Exploding plaque in a blood vessel in the brain leads to a stroke. Exploding plaque in the heart leads to a heart attack.

. . . .

A GLIMPSE OF **WHAT HAPPENS IN THOSE FINAL MOMENTS**

Depending on which part of the blood vessel the plaque is when it ruptures, the final moments may be brief. If it is near the origin of the left main artery of the heart (the beginning of the blood vessel), the heart muscle will die quickly. Blood flow will then cease, and the brain will usually stop functioning, causing the person to lose consciousness within three minutes. If the blockage takes place further downstream in a smaller blood vessel of the heart, less of the heart muscle will be affected and the level of pain will vary.

The victim may only have time to yell out for help. Many times the person never fully knows what happened. In fact, 63 percent of women and 50 percent of men who die of a heart attack *never experienced chest pain prior to their fatal heart attack.*

I often wonder what people think when the reality of the situation hits them. I doubt that they think, *Oops, I shouldn't have eaten all those Big Macs and fries*, or *Gosh, I wish I had exercised more.* More than likely, they immediately think of their loved ones and experience an overwhelming sense of despair as they realize that they may not be able to see them again.

I have sat with lung cancer patients as they sobbed hysterically, asking rhetorically over and over, "Why couldn't I quit? Why couldn't I quit?" As a doctor, in that moment I have felt horrible, inadequate and angry that I couldn't have said or done something to prevent the situation. Unfortunately, at that point all I know to do for them is to comfort them and pray with them.

. . . .

Ironically, 63 percent of women and 50 percent of men who die of a heart attack never experienced chest pain prior to their fatal heart attack.

. . . .

IT IS POSSIBLE TO **SURVIVE EXPLODING PLAQUE**

Of those who survive a heart attack, about half will be able to return to their normal activities. They will probably be able to think clearly and experience good quality of life. The other half will be disabled for life to some degree. The range of the disability will be mild shortness of breath to severe heart failure or angina (chest pain with exertion), but their lives will never be the same.

The prospects are not as good for the 685,000[9] that survive a stroke each year. Like heart attacks, many stroke victims die at the time of their first stroke—most of them never having had any previous symptoms.

The best way to understand this event (the process of watching plaque explode) is to go to https://www.nichd.nih.gov/health/topics/stroke/conditioninfo/risk and watch the video.

---

9 American Heart Association, *"Heart Disease and Stroke Statistics, 2009 Update,"* p. 15.

Watching it unfold will help you understand it and connect the role of each component in the process that we have discussed.

....

Of those who survive a heart attack, about half will be able to return to their

normal activities. The other half will be disabled for life to some degree.

....

THERE ARE OTHER **CASUALTIES OF THE WAR WITHIN**

In many cases, those who suffer most from the effects of exploding plaque are the loved ones left behind. Even if the heart attack or stroke victim survives, their spouse often has to endure seeing the one they love reduced to an invalid, and their lives are transformed into the role of a caregiver day after day. During the season of life when many couples expect to be traveling and seeing the world, the spouse often finds him or herself trapped by an illness their partner has. Although the spouse may have warned their partner of their poor choices, they had little, if any, power to prevent them. Consequently, dreams go unfulfilled and hopelessness often begins to take over their lives.

Victims also have children who become casualties of the war within. If a parent dies young, his or her kids will miss out on the love, wisdom and support that could have been provided. A daughter may miss being given away on her wedding day by her father. Grandkids may never experience the love and attention that only a grandmother can give. And on it goes. Indeed, our choices don't just affect us—they affect all those our life touches.

There is an excellent bestselling book called *Unexpected Legacy of Divorce: A 25 Year Landmark Study* by Judith S. Wallerstein, Julia M. Lewis, and Sandra Blakeslee. It shows some of the far-reaching effects of broken relationships. If someone wrote a book titled *The Unexpected Legacy of Premature*

Spousal or Parental Death, I wonder what it would say. Yes, I believe the person who dies with a strong faith in God goes to a better place, but what is the effect on their families that are left behind? I think we can be sure to say that they are profoundly affected. Possibly they can turn the loss into positive motivation to live a healthy and vital life themselves. But having a deep emotional scar that one has to get over is challenging. I know that everyone is going to die one day, but as a medical doctor with over twenty-five years of experience, I can confidently say that too many people are dying before their time. This is what I am passionate to see changed.

. . . .

In many cases, those who suffer most from the effects of exploding plaque are the loved ones left behind. Spouses and children of victims become casualties of the war within. Possibly they can turn the loss into motivation to live a healthy and vital life themselves. But having a deep emotional scar that one has to get over is challenging.

. . . .

DON'T WAIT UNTIL YOU'RE IN <u>TROUBLE</u>—
GET TESTED NOW!

The best way to determine if your arteries contain plaque is to get tested. The science of medicine has come very far in its research and treatment of plaque formation. There are tests you can take to reveal if you are at risk of exploding plaque. Here are a few that I would encourage you to consider.

The hsCRP Test

In Number 5, *Blood Pressure*, we discussed how VCAMs and ICAMs act as "red flags" to call for help when the lining becomes inflamed. As it turns out, there is a test we can have done that measures the amount of irritation, or inflammation, in blood vessels, and it tells us if the process of plaque buildup is occurring in our body. It is called the **hsCRP test**. It is able to detect very low levels of inflammation. Consequently, if the level of inflammation is consistently elevated, we know that the walls of the arteries are a smoldering battleground. Excess energy is floating around in the bloodstream with no place to go.

If this is occurring, work must be done to lower the first six numbers. One side note I want to add: When we get sick with a cold or experience other conditions, like rheumatoid arthritis, the hsCRP test will turn up positive for reasons other than plaque buildup. Your doctor can help you interpret the results accurately.

Additionally, research has shown that if your hsCRP is elevated and you take an 81 mg aspirin every day (a baby ASA is enough), then the risk of having a stroke or heart attack is reduced significantly.

....

The best way to determine if your arteries contain plaque is to get tested. The science of medicine has come very far in its research and treatment of plaque formation. There are tests you can take to reveal if you are at risk of exploding plaque.

....

The Ultrasound Test

Up until now, everything we have talked about has been from the perspective of the outside looking in. We have discussed the importance of getting our seven numbers and determining what is going on in our blood vessels and heart. Now we are going to change our perspective and look at the blood vessels themselves.

One of the most common methods of looking inside the body is called an **ultrasound**. This test is used to view a baby's growth inside his mother's womb, but it is also used to observe the condition of blood vessels. Any vessels that are not obscured by bones can be looked at with an ultrasound.

This includes the *femoral* arteries of the legs, the aorta in the abdominal area, and the *carotid* arteries of the neck. We can look straight at the artery to see if plaque has begun to accumulate.

The CIMT (Carotid Intimal Medial Thickness) Test

The carotid arteries in particular have become an area of increased study lately because of their strategic location in the neck. When exploding plaque occurs in this area, it can be particularly damaging due to its close proximity to the brain. Consequently, another test has been developed for the carotids. It is called the **CIMT test**.

This CIMT test provides a high resolution examination of the carotid arteries. It is a more sensitive test and thus has been proven to be particularly effective in diagnosing and following plaque buildup in the body.[10] Depending on where you live, a doctor in your area may have access to this test. It's one you may want to consider having performed. You can learn more about it by going to **www.thesevennumbers.com**.

The Heartogram™ or Coronary Calcium Score Test

The last test I want to mention is by far my favorite. It is called the **Heartogram™** or **Coronary Calcium Score Test**. I believe using this test has been a real lifesaver to my patients. It reveals the calcium buildup inside the coronary arteries. If you look at the figure below, you will see the progression of plaque buildup in an artery. Notice the circular figures at the bottom of the graph. What is shown here in the wall of the artery is the buildup of plaque, which can be of two consistencies: the soft plaque (shown in grey) and the hard plaque (shown in white).

As the process progresses, there is a growing amount of white within the section of growing plaque. This is plaque that has been *calcified*. This hardening takes place as early, soft plaque that has been deposited into the blood vessel wall matures and becomes more stable. Ironically, calcified plaque is less dangerous than soft plaque as it is less likely to rupture. However, it is believed that in untreated instances, where there is hard, calcified plaque, there is also soft plaque looming nearby. While soft plaque is more likely to explode, both work to injure the function and often block the blood vessel.

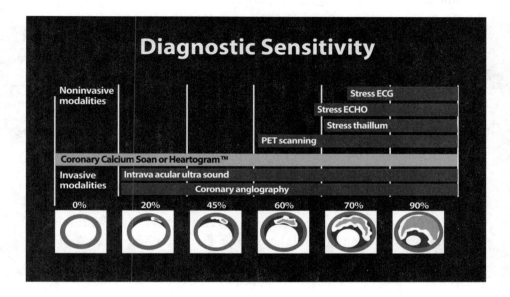

THERE IS **HOPE FOR YOU!**

As I shared earlier, when I was thirty-six years old, I awoke one morning and discovered an obese middle-aged man staring back at me in the mirror. Somehow I managed to be oblivious to the dramatic changes happening during the 15 years when I went from 179 to 242 pounds. I guess I was too busy studying, going through residency and starting a medical practice. I really don't know how a person could overlook the fact they were gaining over 60 pounds, but I did.

Perhaps the most sobering and frightening realization I experienced happened when I turned 40. I had been getting Heartogram™ every couple of years before then, when suddenly, my scan came back positive. It showed

---

11   Modified from Erbel. *Herz.* 1996;21:75-77

a calcified buildup of plaque in some of my coronary arteries. *Holy cow!* I thought. *I have heart disease!* It was an early detection, but it was there. What could I do?

It was in the midst of understanding this process within my own body and learning what I had to do to slow down or reverse what was happening that I came up with *The Seven Numbers That Will Save Your Life!* Only in this case, it was *my* life I was trying to save. I carefully thought through the process of what was going on inside my arteries. I tried to understand how I ended up with heart disease. In time, answers surfaced.

Remember, this was four years after I had figured out that I was obese. My weight was down 50 pounds to the mid 190s. However, I believe the major reason for my development of heart disease was that I was not exercising consistently. Consequently, I still had a BMI of 28 (ideal is 25 or less), and my good HDL cholesterol was 34, which is low. It's important to note that a low HDL level is the number one symptom in men under the age of 50 who have heart attacks. In any case, my overall HDL/total cholesterol ratio was 4.5, which was definitely higher than it should be. Thankfully, this was my only real abnormality. My blood pressure and blood sugar, which had previously been high when I had a BMI of 34, were back down to normal.

REMEMBER THOSE HEALTHY NUMBERS!

A Healthy BMI is less than 25

A Healthy LDL level is less than 70

A Healthy HDL level is greater than 50 in men and greater than 60 in women

A Healthy TC/HDL Ratio is less than 3.5

In any event, it was time to go to work. The first thing I did to get my HDL up was to start taking vitamin B3, niacin. Initially, I started with 500 mg at bedtime and gradually increased this amount to 1000 mg without too much flushing (a non-dangerous, but uncomfortable side effect of niacin). Soon my HDL was up 20 percent—from 34 to a whopping 40. And my LDL was down below 100. Although my HDL still needed to increase and my LDL decrease, I was moving in the right direction.

At the same time, I decided to cut out starchy carbohydrates like white bread, white rice, non-whole-grain pasta, white potatoes, and corn products. Next, I started to work out every morning at 5:30 a.m. with my cardiologist, Dr. John Osborne. He agreed to train with me to encourage and support me on my journey. I focused on weight lifting with a slow "relaxation" phase of the exercises. This is the portion of the exercise that leads to the most tissue breakdown, and thus, generates the greatest increase in HDL cholesterol.

One year later I had another Heartogram™, and guess what? *The plaque in my arteries was gone!* It had been re-absorbed. The HDL cholesterol had gone in and removed all the plaque. The aging process of my arteries had not only been stabilized but also reversed. The science worked, just as expected. That was in 2000. Since that time I have seen the process of stabilizing and removing plaque from the arteries repeated again and again in a number of people. One note: The soft plaque, which is the more dangerous problem, can always be reabsorbed. In some individuals, we are not able to get the calcified, stable plaque to be removed. Thankfully, I caught my hard plaque before it was too late.

My father took a Heartogram™ and had a relatively high calcium score. To confirm the findings, he had a Computer Tomography Arteriogram (CTA) done on his coronary arteries. It revealed a 40 percent blockage in one of his major heart vessels. Immediately, we went to work with his doctor to get his Seven Numbers under control. One year later, the 40 percent blockage was down to a 20 percent obstruction! How fantastic! We have come so far in understanding how this process occurs that we know how to reverse it! If there is hope for me and hope for my father, there is hope for you!

Figure 2 a Coronary Calcium Scan or Heartogram™. The white is the calcified plaque in the study.

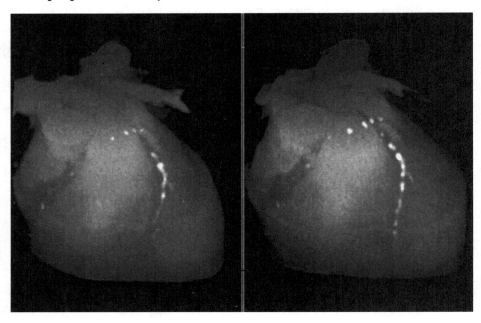

Figure Next. The Computer Tomography Angiogram (CTA) Scan

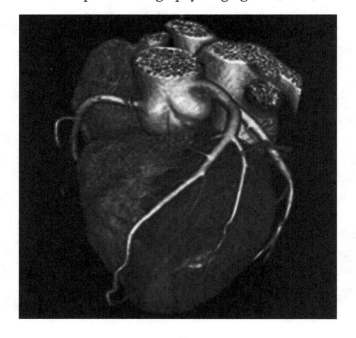

IT'S YOUR TURN TO **SEIZE THE DAY!**

Right now a window of opportunity is open before you. You have a window through knowledge to find out what is going on inside your body—to see if you are at risk of developing exploding plaque, *before* it devastates or ends your life. God has provided you with the wisdom to act before you ever experience the first chest pain. Time and again, it has been proven that when people exercise and eat right, they reduce the risk of diseases caused by exploding plaque.

The Nurse's Health Study is a perfect example of what happens when people hear and heed the wisdom to exercise and eat right. Dr. Hu and his colleagues followed over 25,000 female nurses and monitored their lifestyle choices. They published their findings in a recent New England Journal of Medicine article. The women who kept their BMI under 25, exercised regularly, ate a healthy diet of whole-grain products and fresh fruits and vegetables, did not smoke, and only drank alcohol in moderation, decreased their heart attack rate by 88 percent!

As I said at the opening of the book, changes in your body are the result of a logical series of steps. By discovering these changes, you discover the quality of your health and where you are in the process. In many cases, disease can be slowed or even prevented once discovered. The key is to develop "the ears to hear and the eyes to see" what is occurring. With these newly refined senses, you can seize the day and take control of your health. Are you ready?

EXPLODING PLAQUE: PRESSING TOWARD THE GOAL

RECOMMENDED TESTS	UNHEALTHY	INTERMEDIATE	ACHIEVING EXCELLENCE
Heartogram™/ Calcium Score	**Greater than 100**	0-100	0
hsCRP	**Greater than 2.0**		**Less than 2.0**

PLAYING THE GAME OF HEALTH

5 STEPS TO AVOIDING EXPLODING PLAQUE

AWARENESS: Do you know if you have a problem with exploding plaque? Have you ever had any of the symptoms described earlier? Have you or a member of your family ever had a heart attack or stroke? Make an appointment with your doctor and schedule one of the recommended tests to see what is going on inside your blood vessels.

UNDERSTANDING: Can you see the life-or-death urgency connected with this dangerous condition? Do you understand how the problem of plaque begins and how to begin to eliminate it?

HABITS: What habits in your life are adding to the presence of exploding plaque? How can you eliminate these? Who are you in relationship with that indirectly or directly influences you to make unhealthy food and lifestyle choices?

ACCOUNTABILITY: Who are you in relationship with that encourages you to take care of yourself and live healthy? Who makes you feel that you have value and purpose? Make an effort to connect with these people on a regular basis and be accountable to them with your progress. They are of great value.

SHARING: As you make progress and eliminate plaque from your arteries, journal your journey. You will undoubtedly cross paths with others who are searching for direction and answers, and you will have something to share with them.

CONCLUSION
SOME FINAL FOOD FOR THOUGHT

As we wrap things up, I want to address a question I get asked quite often: "Dr. Conard, is this food *good* or is it *bad*?" Unless you are eating toxins, I believe there is no such thing as "good" or "bad" food. The context of what and how much you are eating is the key. Depending on where you are in life and what is going on inside your body, foods are either more or less likely to help you achieve health.

For instance, there are thin people who eat ice cream and cookies regularly, and because of the exercise they get and the other food they are eating— very healthy food—their body can tolerate these foods without damage. On the other hand, there are obese people who eat a small bowl of strawberries and cream, but their bodies are so fragile, barely hanging on by a thread to their health, that this can push them over the edge into a metabolic firestorm.

Focus on your body and where you are with your health and what you are committed to achieve. Learn The Seven Numbers for your body. Where are you? How in- or out-of-balance are your numbers? Once you know this, then you can gauge what regular consumption of high-caloric foods, like ice cream and cookies, is doing inside your body. Focus on what you want to achieve in your life, what you are committed to. This includes your level of fitness, the frequency at which you eat foods that support or bless your body with lots of vitamins and minerals and fiber, and your energy balance—calories eaten and calories burned. These are the things that determine your success or failure over the long run.

Now you may be wondering, *Dr. Conard, do you eat cookies, cakes, candies, pies, ice cream, fried foods, grilled foods, beef, chips, and pizza?* The answer is yes…but not all at one time, of course. I have actually had people follow me into stores or walk by my table during dinner, just to see what I was eating. I've even had an announcer tell everyone to turn and observe the contents of my plate! But I've never felt ashamed. I love food and I love variety. When I go to Rome, you will find me eating pasta and cheese.

Sometimes I *eat to live*, and other times I *live to eat*. Here's the key: When I know I'm going to eat a high calorie meal, I accommodate and plan for it. I don't like to go to bed at night knowing that my cells are battling back and forth as fat settles in my tissues. So, I plan accordingly. I've done this so many times that my back-up plan for eating a high-calorie meal has become second nature. I would recommend that you do the same thing.

Here is quick cheat sheet that you can follow when you are planning your meals:

If you are **Living to Eat**, you may be eating foods that *increase* your likelihood of having a war occur in your bloodstream while you sleep (metabolic stress in your body). These include…

> High-caloric foods
> Foods with possible carcinogens, such as fire-broiled or grilled meats
> Foods high in fat, especially saturated and trans fatty acids
> Foods high in refined sugar or starch
> Foods high in sodium

If you are **Eating to Live**, you are eating foods that *decrease* your likelihood of having metabolic stress in your body. These include…

> **Foods with a lot of vitamins and minerals.** Vegetables have many colors because of their nutrients. My wife and I challenge our children to eat a vegetable from each color of the rainbow each day. This makes eating vegetables fun and it gives those who are most precious to me the daily benefits of many different vitamins.
>
> **Foods with a lot of fiber.** The average American gets 12 to 18 grams of fiber per day. The recommendation is 25 to 30 grams per day. Fiber is what cleans the inside of our digestive system and moves the toxin-producing, bacteria-laden stool out of our body. In addition, if you eat your fiber early in your meal, it tends to decrease the stress the next portion of the meal places on your body.
>
> **Foods with lean protein.** Protein "sticks to our bones" and keeps us feeling full for several hours. Lean protein contains a lot of good B vitamins and other valuable nutrients. Women especially need to work on eating more lean protein.

Foods with monounsaturated fats that contain DHA and EPA.
Monounsaturated fats raise the level of good HDL cholesterol and
lower the level of destructive LDL cholesterol in your blood. DHA
and EPA are fats from fish. They improve the functioning of our
arteries and prevent further destruction. They also reduce inflammation and promote joint health.

As a rule, I recommend you **Eat to Live**. Eat foods that *decrease* the likelihood of creating a crisis inside your body. At the same time, don't be afraid
to occasionally eat foods that fall in the **Live to Eat** category. Again, it's
about balance, not deprivation.

WHAT IS **THE MOST IMPORTANT MESSAGE YOU CAN TAKE FROM THIS BOOK**?

Given the fact that the everyday choices we make in our lives, our lifestyle
choices, determine what happens to us for the next four to eight hours and
either gets us into or out of TROUBLE, we have a significant amount of
influence over our health.

Be proactive—live the life YOU want to live. Don't sit around in fear, waiting for death or disease to strike. Being proactive about your health and
wellness is the foundation of adding years to your life and life to your years.

The most important message you can take from this book is YOU HAVE
THE POWER to **manage the risk factors of plaque growth**. It is always
easier to "keep the cat in the bag, rather than chase it around to try to get
it back in." In other words, it is easier to prevent a problem rather than try
to get rid of it. The whole modern practice of preventive medicine stands
on this principle. As the old saying goes, "An ounce of prevention is worth
a pound of cure."

OKAY, SO **WHERE DO YOU GO FROM HERE**?

We have certainly covered a lot of territory on this journey. Let's take a moment and recap *The Seven Numbers That Will Save Your Life!* to keep them fresh in our minds. Remember, these are seven primary areas of importance connected with our body's health and they form the word TROUBLE.

T is *Training* – it shows your fitness, based on the amount of activity in your life.
R is *Roundness* – it reveals your Body Mass Index (BMI)—weight in relation to height.
O is *Oil* – it measures the quantity/quality of fat in your blood (triglycerides, LDL, HDL).
U is *Unacceptable Sugar* – it indicates the "sugar stress" levels in your blood.
B is *Blood Pressure* – it measures the pressure on the inside of your blood vessels.
L is *Lousy Habits* – it identifies behaviors that hold you back from good health.
E is *Exploding Plaque* – it exposes the fat buildup inside your arteries that leads to heart attacks and strokes, the #1 killer in the U.S. for both women and men.

By assessing your TROUBLE numbers, you can accurately determine where you are in the spectrum of good health—unhealthy, borderline, or healthy. Now, here's the question:

Where do you fall in this spectrum?

Are you at risk of developing exploding plaque? Are you confident that things are fine when really they are not? The truth is no one is beyond the debilitating grip of cardiovascular disease. All are at risk—from the thinnest to the most obese. I have witnessed too many horrible, pointless heart attacks and strokes to remain silent.

I urge you to find out your numbers. Take an honest look at them and see if you are at risk. If you are in danger in certain areas, begin to make the necessary changes and then recheck those numbers to see how your body is responding. With Roundness (weight), Blood Sugar and/or Blood Pressure, you may want to recheck it daily. With Oil (cholesterol), you may recheck it every three months. And with Exploding Plaque, consider taking the hsCRP test every three months, or the calcium score once every year if you are trying to get it down (or every five years if it is 0). Regularly re-assessing your numbers is a vital part of the process. Don't wait for the government, your friends, or anybody else to take you by the hand and make changes for you. Take the initiative! Find out your numbers. Get in the Game!

Let us know how you are doing on your journey and how we can help. You can shoot me an e-mail at **www.thesevennumbers.com**. If I can educate, equip, or encourage you, I would be honored. To take the next step in your quest for better living, check out the sequel to this book, *The Seven Healers*, at **www.mysevenhealers.com**. Stay in your commitment to living healthy, and may God bless you and your family.

Scott Conard, MD

SECTIONTHREE
EMPOWERING RESOURCES

Calories Used per Hour in Common Physical Activities

Moderate Physical Activity	Approximate Calories/30 Minutes for a 154 lb Person[1]	Approximate Calories/Hr for a 154 lb Person[1]
Hiking	185	370
Light gardening/yard work	165	330
Dancing	165	330
Golf (walking and carrying clubs)	165	330
Bicycling (<10 mph)	145	290
Walking (3.5 mph)	140	280
Weight lifting (general light workout)	110	220
Stretching	90	180
Moderate Physical Activity	Approximate Calories/30 Minutes for a 154 lb Person[1]	Approximate Calories/Hr for a 154 lb Person[1]
Running/jogging (5 mph)	295	590
Bicycling (>10 mph)	295	590
Swimming (slow freestyle laps)	255	510
Aerobics	240	480
Walking (4.5 mph)	230	460
Heavy yard work (chopping wood)	220	440
Weight lifting (vigorous effort)	220	440
Basketball (vigorous)	220	440

1 Calories burned per hour will be higher for persons who weigh more than 154 lbs (70 kg) and lower for persons who weigh less. | Source: Adapted from Dietary Guidelines for Americans 2005, page 16, Table 4.
Source: http://www.cdc.gov/healthyweight/physical_activity/index.html

Body Mass Index Table

	Normal						Overweight					Obese										Extreme Obesity														
BMI	19	20	21	22	23	24	25	26	27	28	29	30	31	32	33	34	35	36	37	38	39	40	41	42	43	44	45	46	47	48	49	50	51	52	53	54
Height (inches)												Body Weight (pounds)																								
58	91	96	100	105	110	115	119	124	129	134	138	143	148	153	158	162	167	172	177	181	186	191	196	201	205	210	215	220	224	229	234	239	244	248	253	258
59	94	99	104	109	114	119	124	128	133	138	143	148	153	158	163	168	173	178	183	188	193	198	203	208	212	217	222	227	232	237	242	247	252	257	262	267
60	97	102	107	112	118	123	128	133	138	143	148	153	158	163	168	174	179	184	189	194	199	204	209	215	220	225	230	235	240	245	250	255	261	266	271	276
61	100	106	111	116	122	127	132	137	143	148	153	158	164	169	174	180	185	190	195	201	206	211	217	222	227	232	238	243	248	254	259	264	269	275	280	285
62	104	109	115	120	126	131	136	142	147	153	158	164	169	175	180	186	191	196	202	207	213	218	224	229	235	240	246	251	256	262	267	273	278	284	289	295
63	107	113	118	124	130	135	141	146	152	158	163	169	175	180	186	191	197	203	208	214	220	225	231	237	242	248	254	259	265	270	278	282	287	293	299	304
64	110	116	122	128	134	140	145	151	157	163	169	174	180	186	192	197	204	209	215	221	227	232	238	244	250	256	262	267	273	279	285	291	296	302	308	314
65	114	120	126	132	138	144	150	156	162	168	174	180	186	192	198	204	210	216	222	228	234	240	246	252	258	264	270	276	282	288	294	300	306	312	318	324
66	118	124	130	136	142	148	155	161	167	173	179	186	192	198	204	210	216	223	229	235	241	247	253	260	266	272	278	284	291	297	303	309	315	322	328	334
67	121	127	134	140	146	153	159	166	172	178	185	191	198	204	211	217	223	230	236	242	249	255	261	268	274	280	287	293	299	306	312	319	325	331	338	344
68	125	131	138	144	151	158	164	171	177	184	190	197	203	210	216	223	230	236	243	249	256	262	269	276	282	289	295	302	308	315	322	328	335	341	348	354
69	128	135	142	149	155	162	169	176	182	189	196	203	209	216	223	230	236	243	250	257	263	270	277	284	291	297	304	311	318	324	331	338	345	351	358	365
70	132	139	146	153	160	167	174	181	188	195	202	209	216	222	229	236	243	250	257	264	271	278	285	292	299	306	313	320	327	334	341	348	355	362	369	376
71	136	143	150	157	165	172	179	186	193	200	208	215	222	229	236	243	250	257	265	272	279	286	293	301	308	315	322	329	338	343	351	358	365	372	379	386
72	140	147	154	162	169	177	184	191	199	206	213	221	228	235	242	250	258	265	272	279	287	294	302	309	316	324	331	338	346	353	361	368	375	383	390	397
73	144	151	159	166	174	182	189	197	204	212	219	227	235	242	250	257	265	272	280	288	295	302	310	318	325	333	340	348	355	363	371	378	386	393	401	408
74	148	155	163	171	179	186	194	202	210	218	225	233	241	249	256	264	272	280	287	295	303	311	319	326	334	342	350	358	365	373	381	389	396	404	412	420
75	152	160	168	176	184	192	200	208	216	224	232	240	248	256	264	272	279	287	295	303	311	319	327	335	343	351	359	367	375	383	391	399	407	415	423	431
76	156	164	172	180	189	197	205	213	221	230	238	246	254	263	271	279	287	295	304	312	320	328	336	344	353	361	369	377	385	394	402	410	418	426	435	443

Source: Adapted from Clinical Guidelines on the Identification, Evaluation, and Treatment of Overweight and Obesity in Adults: The Evidence Report.

HAND SIGNALS OF HEALTH

Palm of Hand	appropriate portion of lean/low-fat MEAT. It should be no thicker than a deck of cards.
Width of Fingers	appropriate portion of CARBOHYDRATES, such as bread, pasta, potatoes, corn and rice. It should be no thicker than a deck of cards.
Vegetables	except for starchy ones like potatoes and corn, these are free food. Fill your plate, but avoid high-fat sauces, butter, oils, etc.

FOR DESSERT

A **SLIVER**	of pie or cake, no thicker than the width of your finger = about 1 mile or 2,000 steps
A **SLICE**	of dessert, about the width of two fingers = 2 miles or 4,000 steps
A **PIECE**	of dessert, about the width of three fingers = 3 miles or 6,000 steps

Extra calories should equal extra Training or exercise. If not, they equal extra weight.

ABOUT SCOTT CONARD, MD

Scott Conard, MD, DABFP, FAAFM,
CEO, Converging Health

Market forces will demand more convenience, increased access, significantly improved quality, and lower cost in healthcare. To deliver on these challenges are best met with innovation, transparency, technology, and accountability. Dr. Conard has spent his career as a founder, President, Chief Strategy Officer, and Physician Executive working to help individules as a doctor and to create the systems and tools to empower this transformation.

Board certified in family and integrative medicine Dr. Conard has been seeing patients for over 35 years and was a Associate Clinical Professor at UTHSCD for 21 years. He has been the principal investigator in over 60 clinical trials, written many articles, and published five books on health, wellbeing, leadership and empowerment.

Starting as a solo practitioner he worked as a leader to grow his medical practice to over 510 clinicians over the next 20 years. In its final form the practice was a value based integrated delivery network (IDN) that reduced the cost of care dramatically through prevention and proactive engagement. When this was acquired by a hospital system, he became the Chief Medical Officer for a brokerage/consulting firm and an innovation lab for effective health risk reducing interventions.

Working with corporations, captives, brokerage firms and insurance companies Dr. Conard has seen what is possible behind the scenes and in the data. Today he is co-founder of Converging Health, LLC a technology empowered consulting and services company working with at risk entities like self-insured corporations, medical groups & ACOs taking financial risk, and insurance captives to improve well-being, reduce costs and improve the members experience.

Through Dr. Conard's work with a variety of organizations and companies, including Dillard's, Varsity Brands, Vistra Corp, National Alliance of

Healthcare Purchaser Coalitions, DFW, Maine, Colorado, and New Mexico Business Groups on Health, and numerous medical groups and systems he understands that every organization has a unique culture and needs. It is his ability to find opportunities and customize solutions that delivers success through improved health and lower costs for his clients.